CO-BSG-360

The Story Behind
Modern Books

Books by Elizabeth Rider Montgomery

The Story Behind
Modern Books

ELIZABETH RIDER MONTGOMERY

Dodd, Mead & Company • New York

PRINTED IN THE UNITED STATES OF AMERICA
BY THE CORNWALL PRESS, INC., CORNWALL, N. Y.

Acknowledgments

I WELCOME THIS opportunity of expressing my gratitude to the authors who are featured in this volume (and to the families of those no longer living) for their splendid co-operation. Without their help this book could not have been written.

I am also greatly indebted to the *Horn Book Magazine* for much material. I drew freely from the pages of its entire file of more than twenty-five years.

Finally my thanks are due to the many busy librarians and competent book critics throughout the country who so generously helped in the choice of titles to be included in *The Story Behind Modern Books*. While I assume all responsibility for the final selection, the following gave me invaluable assistance:

Siri Andrews, former librarian and juvenile editor of Henry Holt Company; Katherine Ashley, Wayne County Library, Michigan; Virginia Chase, Carnegie Library of Pittsburgh, Pa.; Margaret M. Clark, Cleveland Public Library; Mary Frances Cox, Carnegie Library of Atlanta, Ga.; Gladys English, Los Angeles Public Library; Helen Dean Fish, J. B. Lippincott Company; Sue Hefley, Department of Education, Baton Rouge, La.; John Hall Jacobs, New Orleans Public Library; Siddie Joe Johnson, Dallas Public Library; Helen E. Kinsey, American Library Association; Josephine E.

Lynch, San Diego, California, Public Library; Isabel McTavish, Vancouver, B.C., Public Library; Mabel Rice, Department of Education, Whittier College, Calif.; Eloise Rue, Chicago Teachers College; Emily L. Spencer, Calcasieu Parish Library, Lake Charles, La.; Bessie H. Stone, Madison Junior High School Library, Seattle; Ann Willson, Seattle Public Library; Bess Wooten, Los Angeles Public Library; Marian Yakeley, Pasadena Public Library.

Particularly helpful with advice, encouragement, and assistance were Thais Albert, Ruth Calkins, and Ruth Hewitt, of the Seattle Public Library, and Elizabeth Groves of the University of Washington Library School.

E.R.M.

Contents

PART TWO

Fun and Fancy

Note: For *Winnie-the Pooh*, by A. A. Milne, see *The Story Behind Great Stories* (Dodd, Mead, 1947) For *The Story of Dr. Dolittle*, by Hugh Lofting, see *The Story Behind Great Books* (Dodd, Mead, 1946)

PART THREE

It Could Really Happen

PART FOUR

A Long Time Ago

PART ONE

Mostly Pictures

1. *Personal*

DEAR READER:

A friend you make today may be as dear to you throughout your life as someone you have known and loved for years.

So it is with book friends. At your first reading of such books as *Mary Poppins, Smoky the Cowhorse,* or *Little House in the Big Woods,* the characters seem like old friends. And who knows but they may be as dear to you all your life as the characters of *Pinocchio, Little Women,* and *Rebecca of Sunnybrook Farm?*

The classics of tomorrow are being written today. None of us can tell which of the many good books that have been published in recent years will become immortal. But we can tell which ones are well liked so far, and show promise of being candidates for tomorrow's classics.

Like *The Story Behind Great Books* and *The Story Behind Great Stories,* the present book tells you how authors happened to write some of your favorite stories. I do not pretend that the books I have written about are the *best* books, but they are all *good* books. I could not, of course, include more than a fraction of the excellent modern books, so I have chosen those which appear most often on recommended lists for boys and girls, and those which many authorities report to be the most popular with young readers.

2. Part-Time "Company"

Ola — d'Aulaire, 1932

WHETHER OR NOT you have ever been to Norway, if you have read *Ola*, you feel as if you know that country of northern lights and midnight sun. The pictures, more than the story, of Ola's travels bring the land of ice and snow, of mountains and fiords, to life for American children. And that is exactly what the author-artists were trying to do. In fact, they formed a "company" for the express purpose of making such a book.

In the spring of 1931, Edgar and Ingri Parin d'Aulaire were having a vacation. They had recently finished in New York the first children's book they had made together, *The Magic Rug*. Now they intended to paint independently. They wanted to reassure themselves that collaboration had not spoiled their individuality. So they were taking a long vacation, during which each would work in his own way, Edgar on his murals and adult illustrations and Ingri on her portraits and landscapes.

It was natural that the Parin d'Aulaires should choose

Norway for their vacation, for that was Ingri's home by birth, and Edgar's by adoption, when he married Ingri. Both of them loved to get back to Ingri's family, to be surrounded by the young nieces and nephews, to join in the long ski trips which her father led, to be a part of the close-knit, happy family circle.

After a few weeks in Ingri's old home, the two artists went up into the mountains of Norway, to the cabin which had belonged to Ingri's family for generations. This was where they loved to paint, on the shores of a trout-filled lake above the timber line, with dwarf birches the only trees. Here for days at a time they painted what they pleased, Ingri in her corner and Edgar in his, with neither looking at the other's work or thinking about it. And they found that the close collaboration on *The Magic Rug* had not spoiled their individual style.

So the days passed . . . beautiful days with the splendor of the Norwegian mountains spread around them and below them for inspiration, with the wonderful air of the mountain-top revitalizing and invigorating them. How they loved this spot! And how they loved Norway.

One day when they were resting from their day's painting, Ingri stood at the window looking out over the mountains and lakes. She found herself wishing that their friends in America could see all this. Children, especially. American children ought to know what Norway is like. If she could tell them about the fun

she had had when she was a child! Her summers in
the country, her winters—

That was when the idea of a book about Norway
began to dawn on the Parin d'Aulaires. Of course, they
were determined not to make books together if the
work interfered with individuality in their art. Dis-
tinctive style was one thing both artists were bound to
keep.

They remembered their first meeting, in that Munich
art school. Although they had fallen deeply in love,
they had resolved not to marry until they were certain
neither would interfere with the other's career. Well,
they had been sure. They had married. And each had
continued in his own chosen field of art, working alone,
unhampered by criticisms or influence of the other.

Then years later, in New York, they had met Anne
Carroll Moore, whose life interest was good books for
boys and girls.

Miss Moore had looked at the two artists, each so
good in his field. "Why don't you two work together
and give us some beautiful books for children?" she
had asked.

"Work together!" Ingri had cried, aghast.

"Oh, no," Edgar had objected in his grave, quiet
way. "We never watch each other paint, or even see
each other's work."

"You see," Ingri had explained, "we don't want to
become like so many married painters we have seen,
who paint exactly alike. We are going to keep our own
individualities."

But Miss Moore had merely smiled. "Think it over," she advised. "You may find that you can do one kind of work when you collaborate, and an entirely different type when you work alone. And children need the sort of books you two could do. Think it over."

And think it over they did, because they couldn't help themselves; the idea of making books for children took possession of their minds. They both loved children—Ingri loved them because she had grown up surrounded by nieces and nephews scarcely younger than herself, so that children seemed to her the most interresting of all people. And Edgar loved children because he had never known any boys and girls when he was a child, but had grown up in an adult world surrounded by artists. When he married Ingri and was introduced to the young nieces and nephews of her family he learned for the first time what he had been missing all his life, the pleasure of association with boys and girls.

Yes, the Parin d'Aulaires were certain it would be fun to make books for children. But work together? Could they? Well, they could try. And they had written and illustrated *The Magic Rug*.

To their great delight, the D'Aulaires discovered that Anne Carroll Moore was right: in working together, they had found a new technique, different from their own separate ways of working.

In addition, this vacation had proved that the collaboration on the first book had not influenced their own painting. Each still kept his separate style, his individuality.

So now, in the cabin in the mountains of Norway, they could welcome the prospect of doing another book for children, secure in the knowledge that such collaboration would not hurt their careers, if they took vacations between books.

Once planted in their minds, the idea of a book about Norway for American boys and girls grew and grew. Soon both were sketching and painting possible scenes to be used. They traveled all over Norway, sketching. For many months they continued to gather material, traveling, painting, and reading. Edgar's objective view of the country as an outlander balanced Ingri's as a native Norwegian.

When at last they returned to their studio in New York, they were ready for the actual work. Then began the process of selection and organization of their sketches, and writing a story to go with them. Each one had such definite ideas and such high standards of workmanship that they argued constantly. To outsiders, their collaboration sounded like a continual fight, but to the D'Aulaires it was merely the surest method of finding the best way to do the book.

Of course the book had to have a hero, so they made a child as they would like to have him. Thus "Ola" came into being—the happy little Norwegian boy who skims over the hills on skis, right into the midst of wedding parties and other gay festivities. (Strangely, when the D'Aulaires' own son, Ola, was born seven years later, he looked exactly like the "Ola" of their book.)

More work followed, with both members of the "Company" painting and both of them writing—though usually Ingri wrote down what Edgar dictated, plus what she herself thought of. Thus the story of Ola and the preliminary sketches were finally finished.

But that was only the beginning. Now came the real work, for the D'Aulaires always made their lithograph drawings directly on stone, as it was done by famous craftsmen in Europe.

First Edgar drew a key plate on a large stone that weighed 200 pounds—more than he himself weighed. This part of the work was a very ticklish business, because he dared not make a single mistake. But his years of practice in preparing illustrations for adult books had made Edgar's hand very sure. With confident strokes, he drew in black crayon on the stone the first picture of the book.

Another huge stone was necessary for the second picture, and one for each remaining illustration of the book.

When the key plates were finished, three prints were made from each one, on stones the same size. Then Ingri could help. Using the impression of the key plate as a guide, a separate plate had to be made for the printing of each of the primary colors, red, yellow, and blue —though each was drawn in black on the gray stone while imagining color! Think how hard that is to do, and what a lot of work!

But the D'Aulaires loved the lithograph work. They labored patiently and carefully from morning until late at night until all four stones for each illustration were ready. Then at last they were through. *Ola* was finished. The "Company" could dissolve; they could take a vacation and paint, in their own individual ways, the things they liked best.

Where should they go for their vacation? Why, to Norway, of course! Back to Ola's country, to see if it was as lovely as they had pictured it for American children in their book.

Thus Edgar and Ingri Parin d'Aulaire established the custom they have followed ever since: for the making of a book for boys and girls, they form a "Company" in which they work together closely and continuously. When the book is finished, the "Company" goes out of business temporarily while both members paint separately in their chosen fields until the "Company" is called into being again by a new idea for a book.

3. *Soothing Fancy*

Story of Babar — Brunhoff, 1932

BABAR, THE LITTLE elephant, his friend the Old Lady, Queen Celeste, and all the other characters of *The Story of Babar* are beloved by children. It is hard to tell whether youngsters enjoy more the delightful story of Babar's adventures or the charming illustrations, for story and pictures are inseparable; together they make the little elephant a favorite story-book character. But Babar might never have been created if the artist's son had not had a stomach-ache.

In 1930 Jean de Brunhoff, an artist renowned for his portraits as well as still-life and landscapes, and his wife, Cecile, and his two small sons were living in a country house in Seine-et-Marne, in France.

One summer day little Mathieu became ill. Something had upset his digestion.

Madame de Brunhoff put the child to bed. At first it was easy to keep him quiet, but as he began to feel better he became restless. He wanted to get up and play with his brother. His mother entertained him with everything she could think of—songs, stories, games. At last she could remember nothing more that might hold the child's attention. She must think of something new. Very well, she would make up a story.

"Lie still, dear," she said. "I'll tell you a story—a brand-new story. About a little elephant."

The boy smiled. "A baby elephant?"

"Yes, dear," said Madame de Brunhoff. "A baby elephant."

And she went on to tell a fanciful tale about a little elephant who went to town and bought a complete outfit of clothes.

The child was enchanted with the story. He asked his mother to tell it again. Then his brother Laurent wanted to hear it, and Madame de Brunhoff told it once more. Each time she added new bits as they occurred to her.

That evening when her artist husband had finished his day's work in his studio, Madame de Brunhoff told him of her efforts to keep their son happy in bed. She related the fanciful tale she had concocted about a little elephant.

"But that is delightful!" cried Jean de Brunhoff when she had finished. "That would make a charming book, with water color sketches. . . ."

A day or so later the artist showed his wife and his sons some drawings he had made of the little elephant.

The children were delighted.

"Make some more," pleaded Laurent.

"More about the baby elephant," begged Mathieu.

With such encouragement the artist did a few more pictures of the elephant every day and every evening he showed his work to his appreciative family.

When the pictures were finished, De Brunhoff wrote the story to accompany them, naming the little elephant "Babar."

Soon the artist showed the illustrated manuscript to his brother Michel, the Paris editor of *Vogue*, and his brother-in-law, Lucien Vogel. Both men voted it a charming book. Without doubt it should be published, so that other children could enjoy it.

The Story of Babar was published in France in 1932 by the Jardin des Modes. The following year it was translated into English. Soon Babar became known and loved on both sides of the Atlantic.

Thus the story that a mother made up to entertain her little son during a brief illness led to the creation of a new character in the realm of picture-books, and made her husband's name known as an illustrator as well as a painter.

4. The Wrong Ducks Were Right

Story about Ping — Flack, 1933

YOU REMEMBER PING who lived with his mother and his father and two sisters and three brothers and eleven aunts and seven uncles and forty-two cousins? You remember what happened when he wouldn't go up the bridge that led to his boathouse because he knew he would get a spank, since he would be the very last in line?

The Story about Ping is one of the most popular picture books of recent years for small children. Yet it might never have been written if the author had not been accused of using the wrong ducks in one of her earlier picture books.

When Marjorie Flack, who had been writing and illustrating children's books for years, published *Angus and the Ducks* in 1930, she was dismayed to find that some people objected to her pictures of ducks. They were not ducks at all, claimed her critics; they were geese.

Was it possible, wondered the author-illustrator, that

there had been a mistake? She had taken the story from an actual incident; both the dog and the ducks belonged to a friend, and she had told the story as it happened and had drawn her pictures from life. Could it be that the friend's ducks were actually geese? She wrote to her friend at once and asked her.

Back came the indignant reply: "Of course my ducks are not geese. They are a well-known breed called Peking ducks."

Peking ducks! Marjorie Flack had never heard of them. Out of curiosity she went to the New York Public Library and began to read about Peking ducks. She found that they were imported here from China, and were grown for the market on her native Long Island. She was much relieved to learn that she had made no mistake in her pictures for *Angus and the Ducks*; regardless of what others thought, her ducks were really ducks, even though they were not the kind usually seen as pets in America.

Once her interest in Peking ducks had been aroused, it was surprising how often she came across more information about them. One day a writer friend who had lived in China came to see her. During the conversation, Peking ducks were mentioned.

"I've often seen them on the Yangtze River," said the friend. "Frequently flocks of ducks live on boats on the river. During the day the owners let them off to swim on the river and wander on the banks. In the evening a little bridge is put down so the ducks can climb back on board, and the last one aboard gets a spank for tardiness."

Marjorie Flack laughed. "A spank for tardiness! What an idea! But there must always be a last one. Poor duck!" And she felt sorry for the duck who would be the last, wondering what might have caused the delay.

Marjorie Flack enjoyed all that she learned about Peking ducks, but she had no idea of using the information.

A few months later, in the fall of 1932, the author had a telephone call from May Massee, who had been responsible for Marjorie Flack's first book, years ago. Miss Massee was developing a book department for The Viking Press; she would like a Marjorie Flack book for her first list. Would the author come in and talk it over? Perhaps she had an idea in mind.

As she started for downtown New York from her home in Bronxville, Marjorie Flack wondered what kind of a book she should suggest to Miss Massee. She had no ideas at all as yet. But she missed the train and had to take the subway from Yonkers. During the hour-long subway ride her thoughts were busy. The information she had amassed about Peking ducks began to take shape in her mind, and by the time she reached the office of The Viking Press, she had a rough outline of a story about a little Peking duck who didn't like to get spanked for tardiness.

Miss Massee liked the idea, and Marjorie Flack set to work on her story. It was to be a very brief story, but it had to be exactly true in every detail. The author spent weeks reading books about life in China and particularly on the Yangtze River. Working on the kitchen table in her Bronxville home, she wrote and rewrote her story many times, with her small daughter and the Airedale dog romping around her.

Although she was an experienced artist herself and had illustrated all of her own eight books, as well as many books for other writers, the artist side of Marjorie Flack did not want to illustrate this book. She wanted the pictures made by someone who had lived in China, who could make the background authentic. So Kurt Wiese, a popular children's illustrator, who had spent some time in China, was asked to do the pictures. Marjorie Flack made a dummy of the book, with rough sketches to indicate the action for each page. Since she did not know the kind of clothes Chinese children wore, she merely drew bare figures in action. Then she sent the dummy to the artist.

A few weeks later Kurt Wiese brought his first sketches for her to see. Marjorie Flack was amazed when she looked at them.

"Why, you haven't put clothes on the children!"

"No," Mr. Wiese answered. "You didn't have any on yours."

"That was just because I didn't know how to dress them," Miss Flack explained.

Kurt Wiese smiled. "Oh, I see. Well, some Chinese children living on river boats often go around without clothes, so I thought you wanted them that way. But I'll dress them if you like."

When the pictures were finished (*with* clothes on everybody except ducks) the story was tried out with children in the school which Marjorie Flack's daughter attended. And then it was published, in 1933.

The Story about Ping was popular from the first; and it became even more popular as time went on. Soon its fame spread abroad and it was translated into different languages in Europe and South America. Thus the ducks that were accused of not being ducks led Marjorie Flack to write the most popular of all her well-loved books for boys and girls.

5. The Big Mr. Small

Little Auto—Lenski, 1934

WAS *THE LITTLE AUTO* one of your favorite books when you were small? Or *The Little Airplane?* Or *The Little Train?* Then you understand why "Mr. Small" is so popular with young children all over the country and why his fame is spreading around the world. While Mr. Small's activities concern simple things a child knows already, the books give quite a bit of technical information about the vehicles which are so fascinating to modern children. Yet when the first of these books was written, it was considered very daring and revolutionary.

In 1933 Lois Lenski Covey, of "Greenacres," at Harwinton, Connecticut, was a busy woman. As a popular illustrator of children's books, she was always in demand to illustrate the work of other authors. As an author, with fifteen books she had written and illustrated, she had writing of her own to take care of. As wife and mother, she was responsible for a big farmhouse and garden, and the welfare of her husband and children.

Yes, it was a very busy life. But Lois Lenski (she used her maiden name in her books) loved it. She would not have given up a single one of her activities. All were dear to her.

The children, for instance. Of course the two older ones were away at school now, but four-year-old Stephen was very much at home and constantly under foot with his toys and his playmates, cluttering up the house and making it ring with his chatter. But how she enjoyed her small son! She loved to watch him at his play. Always, it seemed, he was playing "auto." If he got out his wagon, immediately it became a car to be cared for and driven as Daddy did the family car. If he played with his tricycle, it, too, was an automobile. Everything, in the hands of a four-year-old boy, seemed to become an auto.

Late one afternoon Lois Lenski was in the living room while Stephen and his friends played with the tricycle in the yard, just outside the door. The mother listened absently to the boys' conversation.

"Yep. She's out of gas. Fill her up."

Sounds of an imaginary gas pump working.

"Okay. Here I go." Realistic sounds of a car motor starting.

Another voice: "Hey! You've got a flat tire. We'd better jack it up and put some air in that tire."

And a few seconds later: "Now you're all right."

The car motor again. Sound of the real tricycle rolling. Then Stephen's voice: "Boy, oh, boy! I'm stuck in the mud. We'll have a time getting her out this time."

In the living room Lois Lenski frowned in exasperation. If she had heard that auto-playing rigmarole once, she had heard it hundreds of times.

"Goodness!" she said to herself. "Don't they ever play anything else? Girls play dozens of games, but boys only *one*—auto, auto, auto all the time!"

As she went into the kitchen a little later to prepare dinner, the artist-author thought about the fascination automobiles held for Stephen and his playmates. They never pretended that their vehicles were alive—they never personalized them. Instead, they always pretended that they, themselves, were driving actual cars.

As her hands worked busily with the dinner preparations, Lois Lenski thought; "Since the boys *never play anything else*, autos must be a major interest of the modern small boy. So why not put it into a book?"

By the time several weeks had passed, Lois Lenski was convinced that a book about an auto would interest children—not a book in which the car was personified, to have thoughts and feelings and go where it wanted to, but one in which a small boy took care of the car and drove it.

In her studio, a stone's throw from the farmhouse, she began to draw some pictures for such a book. She drew a figure the size and proportion of a four-year-old boy, but dressed like a man. Almost at once she named him "Mr. Small." Then she drew a car to fit him, and made pictures of Mr. Small filling the gas tank, putting air in the tires, filling the radiator, and other things that a good driver does for his car.

When a few sketches were ready, she showed them to Stephen, making up a simple story about Mr. Small as she went along. The child was entranced.

"What did Mr. Small do then?" he asked when she stopped.

"I don't know yet," his mother answered. "What do you think he ought to do?"

"Oh, I think he would have to change tires pretty soon, and then maybe . . ."

Lois Lenski filed away in her mind all of her son's suggestions, and at her first opportunity carried them out. So day by day the story grew, with Stephen's enthusiastic cooperation.

Then the artist turned writer and wrote down a simple story to go with the pictures. She made a dummy of the story and the pictures and read it through to Stephen and his friends, carefully noting their comments. Later the book was tried out with other groups of children, in the local school and at the library.

When she was sure the story and the pictures were entirely satisfactory to children, Lois Lenski began the illustrations for publication, making wash drawings in tones of black and gray and red. And at last *The Little Auto* was finished, ready to send off.

But its reception by adults was not immediate and whole-hearted. Grace Hogarth, editor at the Oxford University Press, liked the book, but felt privately that it was too revolutionary to be successful. People just didn't write about ordinary things like automobiles, with no element of fancy or personification. However, it was a charming little book, simple, clear, and attractive, so—feeling very daring—Miss Hogarth accepted it for publication.

Once *The Little Auto* reached the children, there was nothing half-hearted or questioning about its reception. Since Mr. Small was a boy dressed like a man, the child reader could easily identify himself with the hero. His immediate reaction was a desire to be that hero and to do the things Mr. Small did.

The Little Auto sold fairly well from the first. Soon it began to sell better and better. And when more "Mr. Small" books steadily followed, with that capable and versatile man in the role of airplane pilot, sailboat captain, railroad engineer, etc., the whole series soon became what is today, one of the most popular lines of books for little children written in recent years. Mr. Small has become a very big hero to the modern small boy.

6. The Book That Wasn't Written

Andy and the Lion — Daugherty, 1938

YOU ARE FAMILIAR with the old story about Androcles and the lion. But do you know the modern version of that fable, James Daugherty's *Andy and the Lion?* If not, you should read it at once, for no matter how old or how young you are, you will enjoy the rollicking fun of this little book, which is a combination of fact and fancy, and a masterpiece of artful simplicity.

Ordinarily a good book, or a good picture, or any other work of art is the result of long, careful thought and work. Very often the finished product which looks the simplest has required the most work to achieve that very effect of natural, easy perfection. But with *Andy and the Lion* this was not so. In fact, the book was never written at all!

By the late 1930's James Daugherty was recognized as one of the genuinely American artists of our country, and one of the most prolific. His murals covered the walls of post offices, high schools, and Federal Housing Projects in many cities, and his illustrations appeared in

more than fifty books by various authors. Yet he was
never ready to quit or even slow down. Always he
took on more work, and more. His studio was constantly filled with paintings in different stages, from
rough sketches to almost-finished pictures.

One winter evening, James Daugherty and his wife,
a writer of children's books and plays, sat in the living
room of their Connecticut country home. The sound
of the wind outside made their fire seem doubly bright
and cheerful. The artist stretched his long legs toward
the blaze and felt that he wouldn't change places with
anyone. He had everything a man could wish for—a
fine wife, a splendid son, a comfortable home, and work
that he loved. And how grand it was to have a quiet
evening at home like this, and a chance for some good
conversation.

Suddenly he broke the companionable silence. "That
was a good play we saw last week, wasn't it, Sonia?"

Mrs. Daugherty nodded. "Yes. I liked the way the
author built up. . . ."

And she went on to analyze the merits of the current
hit.

The evening sped by on wings, as the Daughertys
remembered and discussed play after play they had seen
in recent years.

At last the conversation turned to Bernard Shaw's
Androcles and the Lion.

Daugherty chuckled. "Now there was a play!"

His wife smiled. "How you laughed at that lion!"

"So did everybody else! The lion stole the show.

Yes, that's a real play—something that makes people laugh, yet gives them something to think about."

Sonia Daugherty studied her husband. How his glowing smile lit up his face, yet how quickly he could sober when an idea hit him!

"*Androcles and the Lion* was a play after your own heart, wasn't it?" she asked. "You always did think it's a fine thing to make people laugh."

"There's nothing better than laughter," her husband agreed. "It's healing, you know. Best medicine there is. If I could make people laugh. . . ." James Daugherty's smile suddenly vanished, and his eyes deepened with thought. Sonia knew the signs that announced the dawn of an idea, and she relapsed into silence.

But the silence lengthened, and it was growing late. "We'd better get to bed," she said at last. "You can work out your idea tomorrow."

Daugherty roused with a start. "What? Oh, yes. Well, you go on to bed, Sonia. I'll come in a minute. I'm going into my studio first."

Hurrying into his untidy studio, the artist snatched up pencil and paper. He must get his idea down. It did not need working out; it had been born full-grown in those minutes he had sat quietly in front of the fire. He would do something he had always wanted to do: tell a complete story entirely in pictures—and that story would be a modern version of the old story about Androcles and the Lion.

Quickly he began to sketch. Androcles would be a boy, instead of a man—Andy he would be called. And of course he would be a Middle Western farm boy such as he himself had been, a boy who daydreamed and loved books and animals and circuses. . . .

The pictures fairly flowed off his pencil. The difficulty was not to know what to draw, but to get the pictures down fast enough.

In an amazingly few minutes he had finished. *Andy and the Lion* was a complete story told in pictures, a story that radiated humor, good will and affection, told entirely without words. Daugherty threw down his pencil, tossed the sketches on his desk, and went to bed.

For several weeks the sketches lay forgotten in the wilderness of the thousand and one drawings and paintings that littered the busy artist's studio. But one day supplies ran low. Daugherty prepared for a trip to New York to stock up. Gathering up his finished work to take along, he came across the picture-story sketches and stuck them in his pocket.

When his business was attended to, Daugherty thought he might as well see if anything could be done with *Andy and the Lion*. Remembering May Massee as an editor with a sense of humor and imagination, and also the rare gift of extracting the best from the artists and writers she worked with, he turned his steps toward the offices of The Viking Press.

Miss Massee took the sheaf of sketches and began to turn them over, one after another. She smiled. Her smile grew broader. She chuckled. When she came to the last one she was laughing heartily.

"You must make this into a book," she cried. "At once!"

"I'd like to," Daugherty replied. "I'd hoped it might make a book."

"We need things like this," Miss Massee went on. "Why, it's an answer to prayer."

Daugherty smiled. He could say "amen" to a prayer like that, all right. With a happy heart he went home to make the finished drawings.

The brush and ink illustrations were soon completed, and also a separate set of drawings for a yellow plate. Off they went to Miss Massee.

Soon picture proofs were pulled, and the book was nearly ready for publication—a book without words.

But the editorial staff were a bit dubious as they looked at the proofs of the pictures. People are not accustomed to reading pictures without text. Most of the editors at Viking felt that there should be a written story to go with the pictures. Would Mr. Daugherty write one?

No, Mr. Daugherty would not. He had never in all his life written anything except personal letters—and as few of those as possible; he had no intention of writing a story.

Finally Miss Massee requested Daugherty to come to her office.

"What are we going to do?" she asked. "Here are your splendid pictures, but no story to go with them. And the rest of the staff feel that we must have a story."

"I thought the pictures told the story," Daugherty said. "I didn't think words were needed."

"I didn't think so either," agreed the editor. "However, the others may be right. One of our editors wrote a story to fit the pictures, but I'm afraid it won't do. Here, see what you think."

Daugherty took the proferred manuscript. After reading a page or two he shook his head. "Too much," he said. "Most of it's superfluous."

Editor and artist were quiet for a minute, thinking. Suddenly Miss Massee exclaimed, "Let's take these pictures right now, you and I, and see what we think should fit each one."

She took up the first picture. "What explanation does this one need?"

Daugherty pondered. "How about . . . 'It was a bright day with just enough wind to float a flag. Andy started down to the library . . .' "

"Fine!" Miss Massee jotted it down on the back of the picture.

"Now this one." Taking up the second picture. "How would this do . . . ."

And they went on through the pile of thirty-six pictures of *Andy and the Lion*. When they came to the last one, half an hour later, they had about six hundred words of text. And the book was complete. It could now be published.

And published it was in 1938, to become a prime favorite with boys and girls—and even their parents. The original drawings were purchased for the Spencer

Collection of rare manuscripts as representative of the American spirit in book illustration.

So it was that *Andy and the Lion*, a masterpiece of graphic art and simple, concise story, came into being —the pictures and the text in half an hour's work each. It is the exception which proves the rule that most works of art require long, careful thought and much painstaking effort. . . . Or could it be that James Daugherty's long years of hard work in painting and illustrating, and May Massee's years of working with children's books contributed to the ease with which this book was born?

7. *From Fun to Fame*

Little Toot — Gramatky, 1939

LITTLE TOOT IS a favorite with small children. The busy little tugboat, irresponsible and happy-go-lucky, becomes a real personality to young listeners.

The parents who read this story to their children enjoy it, too; they not only get many a chuckle from the adventures of Little Toot, but they recognize in the pictures the hand of a genuine artist—a master of his craft. And it is perfectly obvious that the artist himself enjoyed making the book; the pages sparkle with humor.

For six years, during the 1930's, Hardie Gramatky had had a good job in Hollywood as an animator for Walt Disney. It was easy work, in congenial company, under a fine and liberal employer, but it was not work which satisfied Gramatky. He wanted something more out of life than this situation could offer.

Early in 1936 Gramatky made up his mind that the time had come to quit the Disney studios. His contract would expire in June and he was ready for something else. For years he had attended art school four nights a week, and he had spent every spare moment painting—painting what he saw and felt. Now he knew that he must be a painter, not an animator. He would go to New York.

Gramatky couldn't explain exactly why he had come to this decision to give up a sure job with good pay for the uncertainties of New York. He only knew that what he wanted to do was to paint pictures, not make endless series of drawings of certain cartoons. He wanted to express ideas in his paintings—his own ideas, not those of someone else. He felt that the only way he could do this was to get away from California, where he had grown up, and start life afresh in a new place. And what better place for an artist than New York? His wife was willing to take the chance; they were both young and they had no children to worry about.

Accordingly, in June the Gramatkys went to New York. The artist rented an old loft of a studio downtown, overlooking the East River, and he was ready to paint. Of course he knew it would take time to get established as an artist; it would take time to paint what he wanted to paint, and time for his work to become known. In the meanwhile it was necessary to eat.

Gramatky found that there was enough hack work available to provide a bare living, and he sat day after day at his easel in his barnlike studio and painted. But the potboiler jobs were uninteresting, and the life on the river, seen through the window beyond his easel, was more than interesting. It was fascinating. All day long boats went up and down the river—freighters, tugboats, and even liners. It was difficult to keep eyes and mind from the busy traffic on the East River. Gramatky began to draw boats.

During that first year in New York, Hardie Gramatky spent all his spare time painting boats. Soon, as the same boats appeared again and again below his window, he began to feel acquainted with them; he began to feel they had definite personalities, like people, and he drew them like that.

One small tugboat especially intrigued Gramatky. What a busy little fellow he was! He kept darting in and out through the river traffic without a stop, first on one job and then on another. Smaller than the other boats, he seemed to try to make up for his diminutive size by his furious activity. Gramatky made dozens of sketches of this self-important youngster of the East River boat-world.

One evening he showed his wife some of his boat sketches. Dorothea Gramatky smiled as she looked at them.

"Why, you've made these boats into real characters, Hardie. This little tug looks exactly like a small boy showing off."

"That's the way he impresses me," answered the artist. "He has a real personality. All of the boats have; but this one stands out."

"You almost have a story here, in your pictures," remarked his wife musingly.

"I've been thinking about that. Why not a story for children? With a tugboat for the hero?"

Dorothea was enthusiastic. "Try it, Hardie," she urged. "I believe children would love pictures like these."

"Maybe I will," he answered. "Some of these days."

In the fall of 1937 Gramatky learned of the Julia Elsworth Ford award that would be given to the best manuscript for a children's book. The contest would close soon. He determined to write a story about the little tugboat and submit it in the contest.

For the next two days, Hardie Gramtky spent little time looking out his studio window. Instead, he worked over his boat sketches, making the little tugboat into more of a character than ever. Then he wrote a story about him, and named it *Little Toot*. The next step was to paint careful water-color illustrations from his sketches, making each one a picture which would be genuine art and at the same time convey an idea.

When the book was finished, the author-illustrator entered it in the Julia Elsworth Ford competition. To his delight, it placed tenth out of fifteen hundred entries. Not bad for a first try in the book field. It seemed that success was just around the corner.

But when he tried to place the manuscript with a publisher, Gramatky met with disappointment. No publisher wanted it. No one was willing to take a chance on it. One big publisher said, "Children aren't thinking that way this year." For month after month the book met only rebuffs, in spite of its initial honor.

Then one day Gramatky had an appointment to lunch with Charlie Murphy, one of the editors of *Fortune* magazine. The artist took his book along to show him.

Murphy turned the pages of the little handmade book and looked at the illustrations. He smiled, and then he chuckled, and then he laughed.

"Why, this is terrific!" he exclaimed. "You ought to have it published."

Gramatky started to explain that he would like nothing better, but the editor was not listening.

"There's Ken Rawson of Putnam's," he cried, gesturing toward the next table. "I'll show it to him. Here, Ken, look at this." Murphy poked the book toward the Putnam editor. "Publish this book and you'll have a big success."

G. P. Putnam's Sons did publish *Little Toot* and it was indeed a success. About the same time, the author's water-color paintings began to receive the attention they deserved. Thus, by having the courage to give up a sure job in order to do what he really wanted to do, Hardie Gramatky built a career for himself as a water-colorist and an author-artist of books for boys and girls.

8. *It Looks So Easy!*

Make Way for Ducklings — McCloskey, 1941

IF YOU HAVE read *Make Way for Ducklings,* you have undoubtedly noticed how real the pictures look. Mr. and Mrs. Mallard, and Jack, Kack, Lack, Mack, Nack, Ouack, Pack, and Quack look as if they had just stopped for a while in the pages of this book before going back to their customary haunts around the lake. Yet the pictures are very simple, as if the artist had merely trailed his crayon around the paper rather carelessly —as if there were almost nothing to this business of illustrating a picture book for children. Yes, that's the way the illustrations in most good picture books *look.* But appearances are often very deceiving.

In 1939 Robert McCloskey was in Boston, working as an assistant on the enormous murals which were being done for the Lever Brothers building. For such a young artist (he was only twenty-five) McCloskey had done pretty well for himself so far: he had won two scholarships for art study, a sketching trip to Bermuda, and a summer fellowship at the Tiffany Foundation Academy; a book which he himself had written and illustrated was being published soon; now he had been awarded the coveted Prix de Rome honor, which he would go to Europe to receive.

The outbreak of the Second World War prevented Robert McCloskey from going abroad to receive this latest award. He must find something else to occupy his time and his mind. Why not make another book?

As he strolled through the Public Gardens, he noticed the ducks. When he was an art student in Boston several years before, he had watched the ducks every day as he walked to school. In those days life had been quite peaceful for the ducks, but now they were having terrific problems. Now their lives were in danger when they tried to cross the street. A steady stream of cars, boys on bicycles, and hurrying pedestrians menaced the lives of these peaceful feathered residents of the park. Something should be done about it.

Gradually a book began to grow in Robert McCloskey's mind—a book about a family of mallards who settled in the Boston Public Gardens. He began to draw ducks every chance he had; soon he wrote out a rough draft of his story idea.

When he returned to New York he took his sketches to The Viking Press, who were publishing his first book, *Lentil*. His idea interested the editor, so McCloskey went to work in earnest on his new book.

But when he began the final sketches, McCloskey was appalled at his own ignorance of mallards. He had watched those ducks in the Boston Gardens off and on for years, and he was an extraordinarily observant person. Yet he found that he really knew very little about mallards, about their anatomy and their habits. Before he could make his book he must learn more—much more.

So his work began. McCloskey spent days in the Museum of Natural History, in New York, studying the stuffed mallards in the cases there, and looking up in the Museum library everything he could find about that breed of ducks. But still there was much he needed to know.

Next he tried Cornell University. He went into the laboratory there to study mallards. Hour after hour he spent handling their wings, noting how the feathers grew, observing colors and textures. Carefully he compared bills and feet. He made many, many sketches.

The ornithologist, George Miksch Sutton, watched the artist interestedly.

"You really do a thorough job, don't you?" he remarked at last.

McCloskey looked up from the duck he was sketching. "Yes, because I can't draw unless I know what I'm drawing. When I put down a line, I want to know it's *right*."

Sutton nodded approvingly. "I wish all illustrators had that sense of honesty. I like to see birds in children's books drawn right. Too often artists are willing to make just any kind of bird and label it whatever they want to."

"Not me," answered McCloskey, going on with his

sketching. "When I draw a mallard, it's got to *be* a mallard."

With Sutton's interested help, the artist was able to get all the necessary information about mallards. By the time he had finished his study he knew just how they differed from other ducks in the way they looked and lived, in their molting and mating habits. He could distinguish pure mallards at a glance. At last he had enough knowledge to go on with his book.

Knowledge, however, was not enough; he needed living models to draw from. He was living in New York now and could not use those Boston ducks which had given him the idea for his book. Also, he had neither the time nor the money to go where wild mallards lived and draw them in their natural habitat. So McCloskey decided to do the next best thing: he would buy some mallards and keep them in his apartment while he drew the necessary pictures.

Early one cold winter morning, he went to the Washington Market in New York and hunted up a poultry dealer.

"I'd like to buy some mallard ducks," said McCloskey. "Some live ones."

The poultry dealer looked at the earnest young man, with his shock of unruly hair, eyes twinkling behind his glasses.

"Mallards, huh? Well, you're in luck, young fellow. Just got a shipment in from the South. Come on and take your pick."

The dealer led the way to a big crate filled with noisy

birds. He opened the crate enough to reach in and waited for McCloskey to make his choice.

Carefully Bob McCloskey looked at the ducks through the slats. He wanted pure mallards, and most of the birds in the crate were part puddle duck. . . . Oh, there was a pure mallard.

"That one," he said, pointing.

The dealer made a grab inside the crate. The birds squawked and leaped frantically to get out of the way of the reaching arm. The dealer clutched a bird tightly around its neck and drew it, protesting indignantly, out of the crate.

McCloskey shook his head sadly. "Wrong one," he said. "That one's part puddle duck."

The bird thrashed wildly as the man held it by the neck. McCloskey watched pityingly as the dealer started to put it back.

"Wait," said the artist. "I'll take that one, too. Too bad to make it go through all that for nothing." And he took the unwanted duck gently in his arms.

Again he pointed to the mallard of his choice. Again the dealer yanked out a duck, the right one this time. Once more McCloskey pointed out another pure mallard. Another grab; another wrong one, which the tender-hearted artist bought anyway. A fourth try brought up the right one. Now he had his pair of genuine, unadulterated mallards, plus two he didn't want. Now all he needed was a cage and some feed. . . .

Fifteen minutes later Bob McCloskey was on his way back to his apartment with his noisy living models.

When McCloskey opened the door to his apartment, his artist roommate, Marc Simont, looked up from his easel.

"What in the world have you got there, Bob?"

"Mallards. I'm going to keep them here while I draw the pictures for my book."

After one incredulous stare, Simont went back to his work.

"Okay. You'll have to clean up after them, though, if you don't want the landlady on our necks."

The next weeks Bob McCloskey spent on his hands and knees, crawling around the apartment after his ducks with a box of facial tissues and his sketchbook, or sitting on the edge of the bathtub, watching them swim. He made hundreds of drawings of the birds.

By the time he had filled several sketchbooks and had worn his knees sore from crawling, he felt that he had all the drawings of grown mallards he could possibly use. But he was still not through with his work. He needed background sketches; and he must have baby ducklings.

So McCloskey made a trip to Boston. He drew parks, bridges, fences, streets, shops—everything he might need for his book. And then he managed to get hold of half a dozen baby ducklings. He took them back to his New York apartment and once more spent weeks on his long-suffering knees, following ducks around and drawing them. He sketched ducklings in every possible mood, and every kind of position—sitting, standing, stretching, scratching, swimming, and sleeping. More hundreds of sketches.

At last he was ready to make the final pictures for his book. And then his long, careful painstaking work paid off. When he made a wing, or a bill, or an eye, he knew it was right; it could belong to no kind of duck except a mallard. It was a fine feeling to know that what you drew was *right*.

Make Way for Ducklings was published in 1941. Bob McCloskey could sit back and take a long breath. He could feel that he had done a good job and deserved a rest. And when his book earned the Caldecott Medal he could feel that the honor was a recognition of honesty and sincerity as well as outstanding art work.

Boys and girls all over the country loved *Make Way for Ducklings*. Their parents looked at it and chuckled. "These picture books," many of them said. "There's so little to them. An artist can just dash them off in his spare time. I wish I had that talent. It's an easy way of making money!"

9. Fortunate Accident

The Little House — Burton, 1942

Do YOU REMEMBER The Little House that began life as a cottage in the country, surrounded by apple trees? Remember how the city grew up around her until— But if you have read *The Little House* you remember all about it, for it is an unforgettable book. It was made by a person who is an artist with both words and pictures, so that the story and the illustrations blend together perfectly.

The Little House is undoubtedly one of the loveliest picture books of recent years. Yet it might never have been written if it had not been for an accident—a broken leg.

In 1929 Virginia Lee Burton, aged twenty, was in a fever of delighted anticipation. She was about to realize her lifelong ambition at last. She was going to be a professional ballet dancer. Yes, her contract was all signed and her trunk packed. Soon she would be on her way to join her sister, already a successful dancer, for their vaudeville tour. Fame and fortune awaited her, without doubt.

Then came the accident which changed her life. It was not a serious accident, but it meant the end of her dancing career before it had started. Her father broke his leg. Someone had to stay at home and take care of him, and that someone was Virginia. She tore up her contract, unpacked her trunk, and settled down in Boston to the routine of nurse and housekeeper. Another dancer took her place in the vaudeville company. Her ambition to be a dancer might never be realized now; that fame and fortune would go to somebody else.

But Virginia was not one to sit and mourn. If she couldn't dance, she could do something else. Painting and drawing, for instance, she had always loved next to dancing, and they could be done at home. So Virginia got a job drawing sketches for the Boston *Transcript*, and studied drawing under George Demetrios, the sculptor.

Virginia's long-wished-for dancing career never materialized. Instead, she married George Demetrios and settled down at Folly Cove, in Gloucester, Massachusetts, to a busy life as wife, mother, and artist. Soon she added writing to the list of her other activities; she began to write and illustrate picture books for her own small sons, Aristides and Michael, drawing her material from her surroundings. The next few years saw the publication of *Choo Choo, Mike Mulligan and His Steam Shovel*, and *Calico the Wonder Horse*. By

1940 Virginia Lee Burton Demetrios realized that in place of a career as a dancer she was building up a name for herself as a maker of books for boys and girls.

An idea for another book had been bothering her for some time—an idea about a little house. It had started in 1938, when the Demetrios family moved their own house at Folly Cove back from the road into an old apple orchard.

"There," she had said to her husband when the move was accomplished. "The house looks much better now. It really *belongs* there among the apple trees, doesn't it, Dorgy?"

"It's true, Jinnee," answered her husband. "Our little house seems quite at home snuggled under the old trees, away from the road and the traffic."

Then Virginia began to wonder: what had the countryside been like there by the road when the little house was first built? Perhaps there had been apple trees around it then, which had since been cut down. Perhaps there had been no road at first. Maybe it had all been quiet, peaceful countryside around the little house.

As the busy weeks passed, she found herself considering the possibility of doing a book about a little house whose surroundings were continually changed by the progress of civilization, by the growth of the city and the development of transportation. But that would mean indicating the passage of time—of many years—in a story in which the chief character (the little house) did not move. How could that be done?

As she kept up with the never-ending tasks of cooking, canning, and caring for the children, Virginia's mind revolved around the problem. How could she get across to young readers the idea of the passage of time, when small children have no conception of time except as day and night, summer and winter? She discussed it with her husband and with her editor, Grace Hogarth of Houghton Mifflin. At last she came to the conclusion that by indicating in the pictures the passing of days and months and seasons, she might establish in her young readers' minds a conception of the passage of years. And she began to make drawings using this plan, trying them out, as she always did her work, on her own boys.

At first it was very difficult to get her idea across in pictures and brief story, but once she had made a satisfactory start, the book went better and better until it was fairly rolling along under its own momentum. And at last the Little House reached a happy ending, under the apple trees where it belonged. The book was finished.

Immediately upon its publication by Houghton Mifflin Company in 1942, *The Little House* became popular with young readers. The next year it earned for its illustrator the Caldecott Medal, which is awarded for the best picture book published during the previous year. So Virginia Lee Burton, who might have become a famous dancer if it had not been for her father's accident, became instead a famous author-illustrator, thanks to that accident. For if her father had not broken his leg, Virginia might not have met and married George Demetrios, she might not have had two sons to inspire her to try writing stories for children, and she might never have discovered her fine talent as a maker of books.

10. To Banish Fear

Rooster Crows — Petersham, 1945

WHEN YOU SEE the first star of the evening, do you say, "Star light, star bright"? Have you ever counted buttons to see whom you would marry: "Rich man, poor man"? Did you ever hear the old saying, "Rain before eleven, clear before seven"? Or, "Two's a couple, three's a crowd"?

Many of those old verses are purely American; children of earlier generations said the very same rhymes. They are part of our heritage, so should not be forgotten.

A few years ago a couple of busy and well-known makers of children's books took it upon themselves to gather these old American rhymes and put them in a book so that they would be preserved for the future generations of children of our country. And they did it to keep themselves from worrying.

It was during the Second World War. Maud and Miska Petersham were busy, as they had been for twenty years, on books for boys and girls. They had lost count of the number of manuscripts they had illustrated since Willie Pogany first started them on this work by turning over to them some children's books for which he had no time to make the pictures. Now the Petershams were known as two of the best illustrators of children's literature in the country, and in recent years they had gained recognition as writers as well.

But the Petershams were more than artists and authors; they were also parents. Their son Miki, for whom they had written their first book, *Miki*, fifteen years before, was now a flier in the South Pacific. Interested as they were in their work, it was increasingly difficult to keep their minds on it when they were always wondering about their son and worrying about his safety.

One evening Maud and Miska Petersham sat in the living room of their home at Woodstock, New York, listening to the eleven o'clock news broadcast. How dreadful the news was! Another battle in progress. Two more B-29's shot down.

Maud caught her breath. "Miska! Do you suppose—"

Miska shook his head reassuringly, though he was far from feeling confident. "No, of course not, dear. Nothing has happened to him, or we would have heard."

"But it's been so long since we've had a letter! So many boys are being lost! Oh, this frightful war! When will it end?"

Miska put his arm around his wife. "Come on, Maud.

Let's go to bed. It does no good to sit and worry. Miki is all right. Forget the war, dear."

Obediently, Maud went to bed. But she could not forget the war and her fear for Miki's safety. She tossed and turned and could not sleep. Of course, she knew Miska was right; if anything happened to their son, they would be notified immediately. But sometimes there are delays in notifying parents—red tape— What if Miki had been shot down? What if he had been wounded, or captured—or killed? It had been so long since he had written, and that wasn't like him. Something must have happened!

Maud began to tremble. Then she took herself firmly in hand. This could not go on. She could not give way to fear like this. Why, thousands of mothers had sons in as great danger as Miki. Did they, too, lie awake night after night worrying? Well, she would not do it any more. She would get to sleep somehow, if she had to count sheep.

Instead of counting sheep (which had never helped her to go to sleep anyway), Maud began to say silly, childish rhymes to herself—rhymes she had not thought of for years: "This little pig went to market," "Roses are red, violets are blue," "Bushels of wheat, bushels of rye," "Wire, briar, limber, lock," "Bye, baby bunting." And at last Maud Petersham, artist and writer, but most of all mother, was asleep.

In the morning she remembered the rhymes with which she had lulled herself to sleep. She went to her desk and wrote them down. Then she thought of others, and still others. And an idea came to her.

"Why not make a collection of rhymes, Miska?" she asked her husband. "Verses that children know and love? Really American ones. Collect them the way you collect stamps." She told him about her experiment in saying them to herself when she was trying to get to sleep. "And you know," she finished, "I had such a time remembering some of those rhymes! I hadn't thought of such things for years and years."

Miska agreed that such a collection was a good idea, and they began to gather rhymes. They asked their friends, and their friends' friends, for more rhymes, for different versions which are popular in different sections of the country. The more they worked on their collection, the more interested they became. They began to feel that they were doing something worth while in gathering and preserving old sayings and verses which had their origin in America. And their absorption in this task made it easier to keep from worrying about Miki. (Although a letter had come from their son by this time, reassuring them that he was well and unharmed, he was still in danger.)

Soon the Petershams decided to make a book of their rhyme collection. But that meant cutting out a great many. Some involved prejudice of one sort or another —racial, religious, or political. They would use none of those, for prejudice is undemocratic, unAmerican, and this book of theirs would be completely American. Out went all rhymes that poked fun at any race or creed, or derided any political party.

There were enough good verses left. Plenty for a nice book. And of course a book had to have illustrations. Soon the Petershams were at work on the pictures.

As they invariably did, they worked together on the pictures. (Neither had illustrated a book alone; ever since they had started illustrating, soon after their marriage, they always worked together.) It was very handy: Miska was right-handed, and Maud left-handed, so they worked at the same studio window, with drawing tables facing each other. Moreover, Maud was exceptionally good at laying out a page, and Miska excellent at details. Maud was good at starting a picture, and Miska better at the finish. So the abilities of each supplemented those of the other.

The Rooster Crows was published in 1945. The following year it earned the Caldecott award, which is given for the most outstanding art work in a book for boys and girls.

Thus 1946 proved a very happy year in the lives of Maud and Miska Petersham. It brought this coveted honor for the book which had helped them to banish fear from their minds and, better yet, that same year brought their son Miki home safe from the war.

PART TWO

Fun and Fancy

11. *The Mystery of Mary Poppins*

Mary Poppins — Travers, 1934

Do YOU KNOW where Mary Poppins came from when she blew in with the East Wind that eventful day? Do you know where she went when the West Wind carried her away? Do you know how she was able to do all those wonderful things? But of course you don't know. Mary Poppins is a complete mystery.

It is not surprising that Mary Poppins is a puzzle to us who read about her, for she was a mystery to the woman who wrote about her.

In 1933 P. L. Travers, poet, story writer, and literary journalist, was in England, recovering from a severe illness. She had recently bought a very small, seven-hundred-year-old thatched house in Sussex, with a garden which she loved. During her convalescence, Miss Travers spent many days in her garden, drinking in the beauty of the flowers, watching the cuckoos and the nightingales, absorbing the healing peace and the loveliness and the magic which the garden held for her.

One day she found herself thinking of a strange

character who called herself Mary Poppins—a queer person who performed incredible deeds. Miss Travers did not know where this unusual character came from. Was she part of the magic of this garden? Had she been waiting here in this ancient house for someone with a sensitive and fancy-loving mind to find her? Or had she come from nowhere to brighten the long days of convalescence?

But really it did not matter where Mary Poppins came from. The important fact was that she had come. After her arrival in Miss Travers' mind, every day was full of adventure, and every adventure was as strange and as inexplicable as Mary Poppins herself. Day after day, as she slowly regained her strength, Miss Travers stored away in her mind these mystifying and delightful fancies.

When she was strong enough to write again, Miss Travers discovered a strange thing: in her notebook, under the date of 1925, she found the name "Mary Poppins"; just the name, and nothing more. Evidently the name had been waiting in her mind for eight years before the amazing nursemaid had come to claim it.

One day she told some children one of the adventures of Mary Poppins. They listened eagerly, wide-eyed with interest.

"What happened next?" they asked with one accord when the storyteller paused.

Miss Travers drew another adventure from the memory of those convalescent days in her garden and began to relate it. When it was finished the children asked for another . . . and then another.

The interest of her child friends in the odd character led Miss Travers to write down the strange adventures of Mary Poppins. But she had no intention of doing anything with the story.

A few weeks later Miss Travers was visited by a friend whose opinion she valued. The writer persuaded her guest to stay for lunch, and started for the kitchen to make an omelette. On a sudden impulse, Miss Travers turned back and handed her friend the manuscript of her Mary Poppins story.

"Would you read this," she asked, "while I'm preparing lunch? I'd like to have your opinion."

By the time the omelette was ready, the friend had finished reading the manuscript.

"This is delightful!" she cried. "Of course you're going to have it published. Every child should have a chance to read about Mary Poppins."

Miss Travers shook her head. She had no idea of having her story published.

All through lunch her friend urged her to send the manuscript to a publisher. At last Miss Travers agreed.

In a few months the book was in the hands of the printers. It was published in 1934 by Peter Davies Ltd. of London, and by Reynal & Hitchcock of New York. Immediately the mysterious nursemaid became one of the favorite characters of English-speaking children. Soon the book was translated into other languages and the fame of Mary Poppins spread all over the world.

Today children everywhere know Mary Poppins herself, but no one knows anything *about* her except what she tells in her books—and if you have read her books, you know how much that is! Mary Poppins is just as much of a mystery today as she was the day she appeared in P. L. Travers' mind, years ago, in her beautiful garden in Sussex, and probably she always will be.

12. Separate Teamwork

Mr. Popper's Penguins — Atwater, 1938

You've heard of penguins, those fascinating, manlike birds that cannot fly. You may have seen them at the zoo, living on cakes of ice, happy in their zero temperature. But did you ever see penguins living in an icebox in someone's home? Of course not; the idea is perfectly ridiculous.

Mr. Popper's Penguins is an amusing story of a man who kept some of these comical arctic birds in the family refrigerator. Because of its very absurdity, the book is entrancing, and its matter-of-fact style adds to its charm. In fact, it is hard to tell whether the story owes its popularity more to the humor of its situation or to the simple way it is told. Each of these important ingredients was contributed by a different author, for *Mr. Popper's Penguins* was written by two people who worked entirely separately.

In the early 1930's Richard Atwater of Chicago was a busy and successful writer. After years of work as a college professor, he had given up teaching for a journalistic career. For some time he wrote a humorous column for the Chicago *Evening Post* under the name of "Riq." He had been book editor and columnist for several other papers, besides publishing three books of his own. No one doubted but that a long and successful career as a writer lay ahead of Richard Atwater.

One evening the Atwaters went to the movies. The film of the first Byrd Antarctic Expedition was showing, and the whole family—Richard, his wife Florence, and their two young daughters, Doris and Carroll— wanted to see it.

As the Atwaters had expected, they found the show very interesting. It was fascinating to see how men lived in sub-zero weather in a barren, ice-covered land, and how they had made their explorations and discoveries.

But the most interesting part of the film was not the people and their work; it was the penguins, the comical birds who walked around in that all-white country, looking like little men in dinner jackets. With one accord, the Atwaters voted the penguins the stars of the Byrd movie. In fact, they were so enchanted with the birds that they sat through the show twice to see them again.

On the way home Richard Atwater was very quiet. As the others talked about the picture he answered in monosyllables or not at all, for he was busy with his thoughts. An idea had struck him, an idea for a story.

In the weeks that followed, Richard Atwater began the story which Admiral Byrd's penguins had inspired.

It was a fanciful tale about a man who dreamed he had received a gift of some penguins and had kept them in his refrigerator.

For all his interest in the idea, however, Atwater's story did not satisfy him. He soon abandoned it, and the manuscript lay forgotten in a drawer of his desk.

Sometime later tragedy struck the Atwater home. Richard Atwater had a stroke of paralysis which left him completely helpless. His writing days were over. His journalistic career, which had begun so promisingly, was at an end.

Two years passed. Somehow the Atwaters had managed to adjust themselves to the catastrophe which had changed their lives. Then one day Florence Atwater began to go through her husband's desk, to put his things in order. She came across the abandoned manuscript of *Mr. Popper's Penguins* and sat down to read it over.

As she read, she began to chuckle. What a delightfully absurd idea! It was a shame Richard had not finished it. Children would love a story like this, only . . . wasn't it too much of a fantasy? Wouldn't it be better if it were more matter-of-fact, if it were told as if it had really happened, instead of as a dream? If the ridiculous things were just taken for granted as being completely possible and reasonable. . . .

As the days passed, Florence Atwater found herself thinking almost constantly about her husband's half-completed story. The funny little man and his penguins fascinated her. Finally the thought came: why not finish it herself? She had done some writing for magazines; why shouldn't she take this unfinished story of her husband's and rewrite it? Perhaps she could get it published.

So Mrs. Atwater set to work on her husband's penguin story. She rewrote the first few chapters, supplying a domestic background for Mr. Popper, with a family who liked to eat three meals a day, whether the father worked at his business of house-painting or not. A few of the middle chapters she did not touch; they seemed exactly right as they were. (The incident of calling a repairman, for instance, to bore holes in the icebox, could not be improved upon.) But the final chapters she had to make up herself.

When *Mr. Popper's Penguins* was finished at last, Mrs. Atwater sent it to a publisher, signing both her husband's name and her own, as collaborator. Little Brown and Company accepted it at once and brought it out in 1938.

The book, with Robert Lawson's just-right illustrations, was an immediate success. Children of all ages (and their parents) have been enjoying it ever since. Thus, although Richard Atwater's writing career was cut short in its prime, his name, thanks to the work of his wife, will never be forgotten while children continue to read about Mr. Popper and his penguins.

13. Hereditary Art

Five Chinese Brothers — Bishop, 1938

THE OLD FOLK TALE about the identical brothers with such amazing powers has never been better retold than by Claire Huchet Bishop in her book, *The Five Chinese Brothers.* It is not surprising that this should be true because the art of story-telling is hereditary in Claire Bishop's family.

During 1924, in Paris, Claire Huchet opened L'Heure Joyeuse, the first French Public Library devoted entirely to children. This library, which was a gift of America to France, soon became a happy gathering place for the children of Paris.

Claire Huchet enjoyed her work as director of this free library. She wanted to lead as many boys and girls as possible to a love of books. Being very young herself at the time, she felt close to the children and encouraged them to share in the activities and responsibilities of the place. This was their library; they should feel that they had an important part in its work.

Soon it occurred to Mademoiselle Huchet that it

would be a good idea to have a story hour in the library. At first she was hesitant about telling stories herself. She doubted her ability in that line. She could never, she felt, live up to the family tradition of storytelling. Her mother's father had been the village storyteller; he was the only one with an education, and villagers would gather in his home in Brittany during winter evenings to listen to *Chanson de Roland*, tales of King Arthur, and many stirring episodes of Breton and French history. So dramatic were his stories that his listeners hung on his words with bated breath, living the tale as he told it.

Claire Huchet's mother, too, was a wonderful storyteller. She had inherited the talent from her father. She, too, could enthrall an audience with her recital of old tales and legends.

But Claire Huchet had never tried telling stories. She doubted that she could do it well. However, if the children of L'Heure Joyeuse wanted to hear stories, she would try to tell some.

To her surprise and delight, Claire Huchet soon found that she had inherited the family gift of storytelling. She, as well as her mother and her grandfather, could hold people spellbound with her stories. And if the audience was made up of boys and girls instead of grown people, that was all the better, since it was young people she loved to work with.

One of the stories which the Paris children loved best was the old tale about the five Chinese brothers, each of whom had a strange and wonderful ability.

Where had Claire Huchet first heard that story? It may have been told her by her father, who was a great admirer of the Chinese and who had often entertained his family at mealtime during her childhood with stories about the "sons of Heaven." At any rate, the tale had been in her mind for years. She liked it more with each telling, and so did the boys and girls who heard it. Gradually she made it a story of her own.

Some years later, Claire Huchet married an American and came to the United States to live. She was Mrs. Bishop now. Again she became connected with a library—the New York Public Library. Again she told stories to children—American children this time. And once more *The Five Chinese Brothers* was one of the favorite stories.

After several years of telling and retelling the tale, Claire Huchet Bishop found that at last she had the story exactly as she wanted it in English, word for word. Merely to have a copy of it in its finished form, she wrote it down.

One day her husband read the story.

"Where is your publisher?" asked her husband in an American matter-of-fact way.

Mrs. Bishop was surprised. She had not thought of doing anything with the story.

"You must take it to a publisher," insisted her husband. "At once."

At last Claire Huchet Bishop yielded to her husband's arguments, and the manuscript was given to the Coward-McCann publishing company.

As a result, *The Five Chinese Brothers* was published in 1938, with Kurt Wiese's delightfully amusing pictures to help point up the tale. To this day it continues to entertain children all over the world as it once entertained the children of Paris and of New York when Claire Huchet Bishop told it to them herself.

14. *Beauty from Pain*

Many Moons — Thurber, 1943

THE LITTLE PRINCESS was ill and she wanted the moon.
Of course she had to have it; the king always gave her
everything she wanted. But all of the wise and clever
men of the kingdom said it was absolutely impossible
to get the moon. What was to be done?

Many Moons is a fanciful story with a lot of delightful nonsense and some good sound sense as well. It is
the kind of story one would imagine coming into being
while the author was in wonderful spirits and the best
of health. Actually, however, *Many Moons* was written
while the author was as miserable as he had ever been
in his life, both physically and mentally.

In June, 1941, the James Thurbers were spending a
few weeks in their summer home on Martha's Vineyard.

Thurber, well known for his humorous writings and
drawings for adults, was convalescent after a series of
five serious eye operations. The strain of undergoing
one operation after another for six months had been
frightful. Even worse had been the weeks following

ite?

At last he decided to try writing in longhand. His
wife set up a card table for him and brought him several
soft black pencils and some yellow paper.

Hesitantly, James Thurber picked up a pencil and
scrawled a few words. But he could not see them at all;
he would never be able to tell where he had written,
and as a result he would write words on top of each
other. Discouraged, he laid down his pencil. He
could not write, after all.

Absently Thurber rubbed his thumb across the paper. Then his face brightened; he could not *see* what he had written, but he could *feel* it. He could use his thumb to guide his writing.

Again his pencil moved over the page, scrawling big letters, only two or three words to a line. Again he passed his thumb over the paper to find where to write next, then once more began to write. The story of *Many Moons* was begun.

A few nights later, Thurber sat at his table, still writing. Frequently he wrote one line on top of another, forgetting to let his thumb guide him. As he finished a page he threw it on the floor. His wife picked up the sheets, numbered them, read them to him when he asked her to, and put them away. So the story of the little princess and the moon was nearing completion.

Suddenly Thurber began to shake. He could scarcely hold the pencil. But, ill or not, he was determined to finish this story before giving up and going to bed. And he continued to guide his trembling fingers over page after page.

At last, late that night, the author laid down his pencil. The story was finished. The princess had her little moon. Now he could go to bed.

For many months James Thurber was ill. It was a severe nervous breakdown. In order to care for the invalid better, the family hurriedly left their summer home and went back to town. In the move, the manuscript which had been written with such difficulty was left, forgotten, on the kitchen table.

When spring came and the summer house was opened again, the manuscript was sent to Thurber. He was much better by now and his sight was improving all the time. He was curious to hear the story he had written during those difficult weeks, so Mrs. Thurber copied it and read it to him. It still seemed like a good idea.

Then the author sent the manuscript to E. B. White, a good friend whose opinion he valued. White liked the story but considered it incomplete. The little princess went to sleep with the moon, and that was all. There were no problems, no complications.

For some time Thurber mulled over his friend's criticism. And at last he had the solution. When the princess saw the real moon in the sky, what then? What would she think about the little moon she held in her hand?

"Helen!" he called to his wife. "Bring me the card table, will you, please? And some soft black pencils and some yellow paper, too."

This time the writing went better. Thurber seldom wrote over lines, as he had done in the beginning. Soon the story was finished and copied.

Harcourt, Brace & Company accepted it immediately and engaged Louis Slobodkin to make the illustrations. (Slobodkin's pictures were so good that they later earned for him the Caldecott Medal.)

With the publication of *Many Moons*, James Thurber discovered that he had found a new audience and a most inspiring one: boys and girls. Thus the story that was born in pain brought together a great American humorist and the young people whom he considers his most appreciative and alert readers.

15. *Four-Footed Masters*

Rabbit Hill — Lawson, 1944

Do you know Little Georgie? And Porkey? And Phewie? And Father and Mother and Uncle Analdas?

If those names mean nothing to you, then you have missed reading *Rabbit Hill,* and you had better remedy that lack at once. You will smile at Father's pomposity and at Mother's gift for worrying; you will love Little Georgie's small-boy exuberance and curiosity and self-confidence; and you will share the suspense that grips the entire four-footed population of the Hill as they wonder: what kind of people are these new folks? As you read *Rabbit Hill* you will look at the human race through the eyes of animals, and it is an enlightening experience.

Rabbit Hill is a story of the animals that actually live around the author's home. It was written because an editor kept asking for such a story, because the animals came to be real characters to the author, and because he discovered eventually that they, instead of him, were the real masters of his place.

Robert Lawson, illustrator of many children's books and author of several, loved the home which he and his wife, Marie Lawson (also a writer and illustrator), had built in 1936, in the country outside of Westport, Connecticut. "Rabbit Hill" the Lawsons called their house, because of the many rabbits that frequented the grounds. But rabbits were not the only animals to be seen there. Occasionally the owners would see a woodchuck sunning himself on the garden wall. Once in a while at sunrise they would catch a glimpse of a red buck crossing the lawn. Sometimes a skunk would stroll along, a fieldmouse would scurry by, a fox would slink through the bushes.

Yes, "Rabbit Hill" was the home of a great many living creatures besides the human owners. And how those four-footed inhabitants of the Hill complicated the business of running a country home! If the Lawsons planted some rare flower, it was sure to be destroyed by an animal that loved the roots or the leaves. If they succeeded in raising a plant that was extremely difficult to grow in Connecticut, inevitably that plant turned out to be the favorite delicacy of one of the smaller residents of the Hill.

"You got to fence 'em out," insisted the Lawson's gardener, Frank Glynn. "It's the only way to have a garden. The varmints'll take the place if you don't."

Robert Lawson and his wife looked at each other. With one accord they shook their heads. "Oh, no," said Mrs. Lawson. "If we tried to protect our flowers with fences, it would mean fencing the whole place."

"Then we'd never see any of the animals at all," added her husband. "We'd better just plant flowers the animals don't like and give up trying to grow the ones they bother."

Frank Glynn grumbled, but he bowed to superior orders and concentrated on raising hardy if unspectacular flowers.

Vegetables were even more of a problem than flowers. Lettuce, carrots, string beans—everything the Lawsons planted—made excellent meals for the animal inhabitants of their place, but there was seldom anything left over for the human residents.

"If you won't fence, you got to trap," argued Frank Glynn. "Let me set a couple of traps. I'll catch those rabbits that have been stealing our lettuce. Fat young rabbits make mighty good eating, you know."

The Lawsons shuddered. "Eat our rabbits!" cried Marie. "Oh, no! Anyway, if you trap a few of them, won't the others be afraid to come near the place?"

"Sure," answered the gardener. "That's the idea. We'll soon scare off the pests."

Rob Lawson remembered how he often paused when he was working in his studio to watch a rabbit hopping across the lawn. He loved watching them. They seemed so unhurried, so happy, as if they belonged there. And so they did. The place was called "Rabbit Hill." If they frightened all the rabbits away—

"It's hardly worth while raising vegetables," he observed. "Our neighbors always seem to have more than they can use. We might as well be friendly and take what they offer, in place of bothering to raise a vegetable garden ourselves."

Frank Glynn muttered and grumbled, but he left the vegetable garden alone and the animals finished it off in peace.

Even the matter of a lawn was difficult. Every time the gardener managed to get the lawn smooth and neat, moles immediately tore it up again with their tunnels.

"If you'd only let me put out some poison!" fumed Frank Glynn. "I'd get rid of those pesky moles in a hurry."

But of course he knew the Lawsons would never allow poison. So he began to stalk the moles. Armed with a sharp spade, he would go out on the lawn at high noon. He would stand perfectly still until he saw a spot of lawn begin to hump and quiver. That meant that a mole was working. Very quietly Frank would move toward the hump, one step at a time. When the hump stopped quivering, Frank stopped moving. When it began to move again, he would take another step. At last, when he got just behind the spot where the mole was working, he would plunge the spade quickly into the ground and bring up a spadeful of dirt *and* the mole. Then one hard smack with the spade, and the mole was still; he would never dig up another lawn.

Frank Glynn finished off several moles that way and kept the lawn of "Rabbit Hill" very nice and smooth for weeks. But one day Rob Lawson decided to see for himself how this stalking business was done. Under his gardener's directions, he armed himself with a spade and followed Frank Glynn's footsteps. It was very exciting. Lawson enjoyed it immensely—until it came to that final blow with the spade. That changed everything. One second there was a beautiful furry creature scrambling around there on the ground, and the next instant the little thing was still. No, stalking moles was not the way to have a nice lawn if it meant killing something at the end of the hunt.

But it soon occurred to Lawson that it was not necessary to kill the mole when you caught it. Why not just take it down the road a piece and turn it loose? Then it would find some other place to work instead of the lawn on "Rabbit Hill!"

Frank Glynn fumed, but after that all the moles which were caught were given a ride in the car and turned loose unharmed.

Yes, the four-footed inhabitants of "Rabbit Hill" really complicated the business of running a country home. However, Robert and Marie Lawson finally got matters adjusted and everything worked smoothly. The deer and the skunks and the foxes still wandered through the grounds, and the rabbits hopped across the lawn whenever they felt like it, and nobody was unhappy—except maybe Frank Glynn, the gardener.

Then one winter day in 1942 Rob Lawson decided to write a book about the animals he saw from his window. For years the editor at The Viking Press who had published his last book, had been urging him to do a book about his rabbits. For years he had refused, but now— Well, it was time to begin a new book, and maybe it might just as well be about the animals of "Rabbit Hill" as anything else. There were certainly plenty of them to write about. That impudent young rabbit who had been romping around the lawn this very morning, for instance; like all small boys, he must give his mother plenty of bad moments. That fieldmouse they had seen looking through the window the other night, attracted to the window sill by birdseed; what if he had fallen in the rain barrel? That pair of old rabbits who had been nibbling the grass in front of the house last week; they looked for all the world as if they were complaining about the quality of the grass. And that skunk who *would* get into the garbage pail. . . . Yes, there were plenty of animals to write about and he might as well begin.

So *Rabbit Hill* was begun. And Robert Lawson found, to his amazement, that all he had to do was start the book, for after that it practically wrote itself. Little Georgie, Father, Mother, Uncle Analdas, Phewie, and all the rest of the characters came to life and carried the story along to its happy ending.

Then Lawson began work on the pictures. They, too, went easily and smoothly, partly because of his long experience in illustration and partly because he had watched the animals around "Rabbit Hill" so closely and sympathetically for years.

Thus Viking's delighted editor finally got the book she wanted about the rabbits on "Rabbit Hill" and it was published in 1944.

Rabbit Hill was popular from the start. It had a big

advance sale and the following year received the New-bery Award as the most outstanding book for children during the year of its publication.

Thus in relinquishing his place as master of "Rabbit Hill," Robert Lawson found compensation not only in the pleasure of watching the animal-masters, but in the profit and fame brought by his book about them.

16. As American as Hot-Dogs

Paul Bunyan, 1924-1936

AMERICANS ENJOY EXAGGERATIONS. The tall tale is characteristic of American humor. Davy Crockett, John Henry, Pecos Bill, Johnny Appleseed and Paul Bunyan are all products of our American love of the "bigger and better."

While all these legendary heroes are dear to our hearts, none has inspired more books than Paul Bunyan, the superlogger of the north woods. His biographers are legion. They come from all walks of life. The best known include a lumberman, a college professor, a traveling salesman, and a designer of lighting fixtures.

During the first World War James Stevens was in France with the 3rd Oregon National Guard. Like most American soldiers away from home, *Stars and Stripes* ranked next to letters from home as his favorite reading matter.

Stevens was surprised one day to see in *Stars and Stripes* a letter to the editor about Paul Bunyan, the greatest lumberman of all times. He was still more sur-

prised when other letters followed, relating more ex-
ploits of the mythical giant. Why, Stevens had heard
those Paul Bunyan stories for years in the logging camps
of the Pacific Northwest. It had never occurred to him
that they might be new or interesting to other people.

When the war was over James Stevens returned to
Oregon and soon he was again working in the logging
industry, this time as a sorter in a sawmill.

One evening in 1923 as he was reading a magazine
called *Smart Set*, he noticed that H. L. Mencken and
George Jean Nathan were leaving the magazine as
editors. Stevens was disappointed. Without those two,
Smart Set would not be the same. On the inspiration
of the moment, James Stevens wrote a letter to Mencken, telling him how much he enjoyed his literary
style.

Back came a letter from Mencken, thanking the
young logger. If Stevens wanted to read more of
Mencken's writings, he could get the new magazine,
American Mercury, which the two erstwhile *Smart Set*
editors were starting. And why didn't Stevens write a
contribution for the new magazine?

James Stevens could not ignore that invitation.
Though he had received little formal schooling, he had
supplemented his education by constant reading and had
always felt a half-recognized desire to write. So he
composed an article comparing the laborer of the old
West to that of the new; the substance of his argument
was that modern life had emasculated the everyday
Westerner.

Mencken liked the article. He asked the budding author to try another. But Stevens had no more ideas for articles. He had said his say in the first one. What should he write about now?

Then he remembered the interest the old Paul Bunyan yarns had aroused among the American soldiers in France. Perhaps one of those might do for Mencken's magazine. It wouldn't hurt to try.

That was the beginning of James Stevens' career as Paul Bunyan's biographer. The first article led to another, then to a series, and finally to a book for adults called *Paul Bunyan*, which was published in 1925 by Alfred Knopf. And after writing many other books and stories, Stevens wrote a second Paul Bunyan book, this time for children, called *Paul Bunyan's Bears*, published in 1947.

In 1920, while James Stevens was working in Oregon sawmills, Esther Shephard, a graduate of the University of Washington, was in Seattle, working for her Master's degree. As part of her course she had chosen a seminar in American literature taught by Professor V. L. O. Chittick.

One day during the course, Professor Chittick mentioned Van Wyck Brooks' indictment of the frontier as revealed in his book, *The Ordeal of Mark Twain*.

"It would be interesting," he said, "to know what the frontiersmen themselves thought of the frontier. What did they think of their way of life, their standards of conduct? How did they judge themselves? It might be well worth while for someone to undertake such a study."

Professor Chittick's suggestion appealed to Esther Shephard. She determined to undertake the study and find out what the frontiersmen had thought of themselves and the frontier.

In the course of her research on this subject, she came across the Paul Bunyan legend in many sources. Among these were a review by Constance Rourke in the *New Republic;* articles by Lee J. Smits in the *Seattle Star* in 1920, and the letters from readers his articles inspired; the chap-book, *Paul Bunyan Comes West,* by Ida Turney and her students; and the advertising booklets by the Red River Lumber Company, written by W. B. Laughead.

Soon Mrs. Shephard became an avid collector of Paul Bunyan stories. She and her husband went into the logging camps and heard stories from old-timers who claimed to have worked with Paul or knew someone who had.

And when she came to write down the stories, she adopted the style that the loggers themselves had used in telling the tales to her—an intimate, vigorous style which has the flavor of the big woods.

Esther Shephard's book, *Paul Bunyan,* was published in 1924 in Seattle, and about a year later in New York by Harcourt, Brace and Company. It proved very popular with young people.

While James Stevens and Esther Shephard were collecting and writing Paul Bunyan stories, a traveling salesman was hearing these old tales for the first time.

In his travels over the country as salesman for a publishing house, Wallace Wadsworth became interested in the legends he was hearing in different parts of the country about Paul Bunyan, the mightiest logger of them all. In the Michigan woods and in the forests of the Pacific Northwest, Paul Bunyan was a hero. Practically every geographic landmark was attributed to him. He had dug Puget Sound; he had made the lakes of Minnesota; he was responsible for the Grand Canyon and the high tides of Labrador.

Wadsworth enjoyed these fantastic tales so much that he began to collect them and write them down in simple enough style for children to enjoy. His book, *Paul Bunyan and His Great Blue Ox*, was published by Doubleday in 1926, and extended the fame of Paul Bunyan among boys and girls.

In 1914 a boy called Dell McCormick was working as log scaler in a sawmill in northern Idaho.

One day a writer appeared in camp. He was going to do an article on the logging industry for *The Saturday Evening Post* and he wanted to see every phase of the work. Dell McCormick was appointed guide for the writer, to show him around and answer his questions.

In order to prolong his pleasant work as guide, McCormick began to tell the writer some of the old Paul Bunyan legends which were current around the camp. The visitor was interested. He kept asking for more stories of the great logger, and Dell was glad to oblige.

When the writer left, he thanked the boy for his help. "Be sure and watch for my article," he said. "You'll be mentioned in it."

Week after week, Dell McCormick scanned *The Saturday Evening Post,* looking for the writer's name. At last he found the article and he read it eagerly.

To the boy's chagrin, there was only one mention of himself. It was at the very end of the article: "When the logs finally reach the mill, they are measured by a very small boy with a very long stick."

Another unexpected thing about the article was the small space which was devoted to the logging industry. For the most part the writer had concentrated on the stories of Paul Bunyan which his young guide had told him.

For the first time, Dell McCormick realized that in his store of Paul Bunyan stories he might have something worth writing and publishing. Immediately he began to make notes of all the stories he knew and to collect others from the men he worked with.

Before McCormick got around to writing up his notes, the United States entered the first World War and McCormick found himself in the army. Writing was forgotten.

Twenty years passed before McCormick finally wrote his Paul Bunyan tales. By that time several books of the stories had been published. McCormick saw first one and then another. Others writers had beaten him to it!

Then it occurred to him that the Paul Bunyan yarns would make splendid stories for young children. That was one field the other Paul Bunyan writers had not covered. James Stevens had written for adults, Esther Shephard for young people, Wallace Wadsworth for older children, but no one had written a book simple enough for young children. That, then, was what he would do.

In 1936 Dell McCormick's book, *Paul Bunyan Swings His Ax*, was published by the Caxton Press, and the entire field of readers was covered. Now there is a Paul Bunyan book for every age except the nursery!

PART THREE

It Could Really Happen

17. *Thrown into Writing*

Smoky, the Cowhorse — James, 1926

PROBABLY NO BOOK about an animal has been more universally popular with young and old than *Smoky, the Cowhorse*. This sympathetic, yet unsentimentalized, story of the life of a horse has made a permanent place for itself in the hearts of Americans, for it not only presents an unforgettable animal character but it offers a picture of life on our Western frontier which has largely disappeared.

Like *Black Beauty*, the horse classic of an earlier day, *Smoky, the Cowhorse* was written to make people appreciate the loyal, intelligent, hard-working animal who has been such a faithful friend and helper to the human race. Yet *Smoky* might never have been written if the author had not been literally *thrown* into writing.

It was the year 1920. Will James, cowboy and amateur artist, was twenty-eight years old. Practically all of those twenty-eight years had been spent on horseback, for he had learned to ride almost as soon as he had learned to walk. And everything he had done since he was left to his own resources at the age of thirteen had been connected with horses: he had drifted all over the West as cowhand, expert rider, rodeo performer, actor in Western motion pictures; even his service in the Army during the first World War had been spent as a mounted scout. All his life he had been riding; he could not imagine any other life.

And yet all his life Will James had been drawing, too. From the time he could hold a pencil he had drawn pictures whenever he could find something to draw on. (Paper was scarce on the range.) Always he drew from memory, and his memories were usually of horses. Sometime, he thought, he might make some money from his pictures. People had often told him so.

One day Will James was on his way North, riding one horse and leading a pack horse; everything he had in the world was right there on those two horses. He was thinking it was time he quit this wandering life and settled down. He would head on North and find some place where he wanted to live and build a cabin and corrals.

But one night he happened to stop in a town which was getting ready for a big rodeo. James was offered a job gathering bucking horses and range steers for the rodeo. He could use the money, so he accepted. Will James loved rodeos. A few years back he would have been one of the star performers; but several bad falls from bucking horses had left him with injuries which prevented him from riding wild broncos. Nowadays he stuck to gentler horses.

During the days of preparation for the rodeo, James became well acquainted with the rodeo manager and began to feel at home in his office. There were plenty of pencils and pads of blank paper in the manager's office, and the amateur artist could not resist the opportunity for making sketches of bucking horses—his favorite subject.

One day Will James came back to the office after finishing a job, to find the manager studying one of his sketches.

The manager looked up and grinned. "This horse is sure tearing loose," he said. "Wonder who made this picture?"

"I did," James replied.

"You? I didn't know you could draw. Well!" The manager relapsed into a study. Suddenly he said, "If you can draw like that, maybe you can make me a picture that will do for a poster to advertise the rodeo."

"Sure," said Will James, and he picked up a pencil.

He made three pictures. The manager chose the third one, and handed him a check for fifty dollars.

Will James looked at the check in amazement. Fifty dollars for one drawing! Why, maybe he really could make money from his pictures. . . . Some day.

When the rodeo was over, the manager suggested to James that a book might be made of his drawings of range life. If the cowboy-artist would turn out about twenty good sketches, he would take them to a publisher friend of his and see about having them printed.

Immediately James set to work in earnest on the

drawings. Soon they were finished. They were the best he had ever made, he was sure, and the manager thought so, too.

But weeks passed and the manager did nothing about getting in touch with his publisher friend. Will James began to be restless. Of course he was having a good time with a couple of cowboy friends who were in town, but he was spending all his money while he waited for something to be done with his drawings.

Finally he decided he could wait no longer. The manager would never keep his word. He might as well ride on North and look for the spot where he wanted to settle. He told his two friends about his decision.

"Aw, now, don't rush off," begged one of the cowboys. "Come on with us, Will. We'll get a job with some outfit and make up for the money you've spent in town."

"Sure," agreed the other friend. "We'll stick in town a day or so longer and celebrate a bit, and then we'll light out for the range."

"Well-ll." Will James hesitated. He ought to be heading for the country where he had decided he was going to settle down. But, then, a few months wouldn't matter, and if he stayed with these fellows and worked a while he would have some money with which to start out for himself. He decided to go with them.

On the last day of their stay in town, the cowboys borrowed three bucking horses that had been used in the rodeo and put on a private bucking-horse exhibition outside of the town, by way of final celebration. Although Will James had quit riding bucking horses, he thought he would try it just once more, since it was only for fun.

James was the first one to ride. He laughed as he pulled the blind off his horse's eyes. This was fun! How he loved to ride! And there was nothing like a bucking horse for sheer excitement. Anybody could ride a gentle horse, but it took a real rider to stick on through wicked jumps like these.

At last it seemed that the horse was through. James got ready to jump from his mount. Just as he was half off, the horse bucked again. The cowboy was thrown against the railroad track and the horse stepped on him.

For many weeks Will James lay in the hospital. He was lucky to be alive. But he would never ride a bucking horse again. In fact, it would be some time before he could ride at all.

In the meanwhile he must earn some money. Doctor bills were mounting and must be paid, some way. Since he could no longer make his living as a cowboy, he would see what he could do at drawing, as soon as he was strong enough to sit up.

During his convalescence, Will James met a man who knew the editor of a big magazine in the East and was given a letter of introduction to the editor. His cowboy friends scraped up money enough for his fare to New York, and soon he was on his way.

It took time and persistence for the untutored cowboy from the West to interest New York editors in his work. Eventually, however, by writing little sketches to go with his drawings, Will James began to get things published. His writing, like his drawing, was individual, untrained; but for that very reason it caught attention. Soon he was writing and illustrating books.

While in New York Will James began to notice that horses were all but forgotten. People were using and depending on automobiles and airplanes. They did not remember the part horses had played in the early days of our country. To a man who had lived and worked with horses all his life, and loved them as much as others love their families, that was all wrong. People should be made to see that a good horse is a wonderful animal—a fine friend.

That horse Smoky, for instance, which he had had for so long. There was a horse! What a lot the two of them had been through together! Smoky was a loyal and true friend.

Suddenly James decided he would write a story about Smoky. He would make it fiction, but everything in it would be really true, just the same. If he could bring Smoky to life, not as a storybook horse, but as he really was, then people would know what a great animal a horse is.

So *Smoky, the Cowhorse* was written and illustrated, with plenty of drawings from memory, by the author. In April, 1926, it began to run as a serial in *Scribners' Magazine*, and then was published as a book.

At once, readers took Smoky to their hearts. The book won the Newbery Medal for the year of its publication. And Will James was very happy. Although that bucking horse had thrown him out of the work he loved—riding—it had also thrown him into work he loved almost as much: writing about horses and drawing them.

18. *Hunter without a Gun*

Bambi — Salten, 1928

CHILDREN THE WORLD over know and love *Bambi*. This beautiful story of the life of a deer has been translated into many languages, including Hebrew and Chinese. It was written by an Austrian Jew who had a boundless sympathy and understanding for the weak and the oppressed; and it was written because the author loved to hunt—without a gun.

In 1919 Felix Salten was recognized in his own country as a writer of ability, but his long career as a journalist, theatre critic, essayist and novelist had attracted little attention outside of his native Austria. He pursued his quiet way, writing for the *Neue Freie Presse* of Vienna, working on his novels and plays and enjoying his family—his wife Ottilie and his growing son and daughter.

One day Salten accompanied, as he often did, a group of hunters into the forests not far from Vienna. The rest of the party carried guns and ammunition; they were eager for the sport of killing. But Salten carried no weapons; he went into the forest empty-handed, for he loved to watch animals, not to kill them.

As the day wore on, he saw many wild animals: beautiful deer, squirrels, hares, and many different kinds of birds. How lovely they were—and how helpless in the face of the weapons of men! What must be the feelings of those animals when a gun exploded in their hearing! How they must fear and hate men!

During many such hunting trips, Felix Salten watched animals and wondered what they felt and what they thought—if they could think. Often he walked alone in the forests and surprised does with their fawns, young bucks fighting, groups of deer grazing or drinking from a stream. Always it saddened him to see how frightened they became when they discovered his presence. Why, he would not harm them for the world! Yet because he was a man they feared him.

At last Salten decided to write a story about animals. He would write about the life of a deer, and into it he would put the tragedy that is inherent in the lives of wild creatures—the constant fear of the hunted.

So *Bambi* was written. Felix Salten's own children loved the story. Then in 1923 it was published, and children all over Austria took it to their hearts.

Five years later, the fame of *Bambi* had spread abroad and the book was brought out in England and in America. Immediately it became as popular with English-speaking children as it had been with Austrian readers.

So the name of Felix Salten eventually reached beyond his native Austria, not through his novels or essays but through the book he was impelled to write by his many experiences in hunting without a gun.

19. Work That Made Work

Little Pear — Lattimore, 1931

LITTLE PEAR TELLS of the everyday life of an average little Chinese boy who, as he grows, gradually learns to be good. Its story and illustrations give a clear and sympathetic picture of life and people in North China, particularly of the lovable and mischievous Little Pear.

This book about China was written in the United States by an American who had spent the formative years of her life in China; and it was written because she could not get work in her chosen field.

All of her life Eleanor Frances Lattimore had dreamed of being an artist. As far back as she could remember, Eleanor and one of her sisters had devoted their spare time to painting and drawing. During their childhood in China they had covered every available blank space with pictures of boys and girls. Blackboards, notebooks and odd scraps of paper were filled with sketches of the various Chinese children who frequented the University grounds at Peiyang where they lived. As they studied their lessons in the living room of their home (the Lattimore children never went to school, but were taught by their parents), they drew from memory Chinese youngsters they had seen in the near-by town.

After the family's return to the United States, the two sisters went to art school. And now, in 1929, Eleanor was in New York, ready to be what she had always wanted to be—an artist. She was going to illustrate books.

But something was wrong. Eleanor was ready for work, but the work was not ready for Eleanor; she could find no books to illustrate. Although she went the rounds of the publishing houses, always she met the same response: "No, we have no work for you right now."

The young artist began to get desperate. She had to have work! Oh, of course she could go home to her family in Hanover, New Hampshire. But that would mean admitting failure in her chosen profession, and failure was unthinkable. She *would* be an artist.

One day Eleanor Lattimore, with her portfolio of sketches under her arm, went to the publishing offices of Harcourt, Brace and Company and talked to the juvenile editor, Elisabeth B. Hamilton.

It was the same story. Mrs. Hamilton looked at the sketches, admired them, and then shook her head.

"Your work is nice, Miss Lattimore, but I have no work for you right now. I'm sorry."

Discouraged, Eleanor started to put the drawings

back in her portfolio. But Mrs. Hamilton had picked up a couple and was looking at them again.

"These little Chinese children," she said. "I like them. They look real."

"I was born in China," the artist explained. "I lived there until I was sixteen. And I have always loved to draw Chinese youngsters."

The editor studied the young artist thoughtfully. "Why don't you write a story?" she asked at last. "A story about a child such as the ones you have in these sketches. A realistic story about an everyday Chinese child might have a good sale."

Eleanor Lattimore looked up, startled. The idea of writing was a new one to her, although as a child she had sometimes made up stories. But if writing a story meant that she could illustrate it. . . .

"If I wrote a story like that and you wanted to publish it, could I do the illustrations?"

Mrs. Hamilton smiled. "Yes, of course. We would want you to do both the story and pictures—*if* we liked your story."

After talking the idea over with the editor a little longer, Eleanor Lattimore went home to the small apartment she shared with a writer friend. She kept thinking about Mrs. Hamilton's suggestion. A "real" story about an "everyday" Chinese child. What "everyday" Chinese children had she known? Well, there had been many such children around the University grounds at Peiyang where her father had taught. There were the gatekeeper's little grandson, the washerwoman's little girls, and the cook's family. There had been the two village boys who used to pick up their balls for the Lattimore children when they played tennis. And there were all the village children they used to see frequently throughout the year as they went sliding on the ice in winter or raking leaves in autumn or going to town on market day. Yes, she had known plenty of "everyday" Chinese children. She should be able to write a story about one of them and tell about his day-to-day life.

So Eleanor Lattimore, artist, began to write in order to have a book to illustrate. And Little Pear, the lovable little boy who liked to run away, came into being. In a week she had finished the first draft.

But the story was too short; it was too bare; she had not described things enough. So she wrote it over, being careful this time to give sufficient detail so that readers could see North China as she remembered it.

When the manuscript was ready, the writer breathed a sigh of relief. Now she could get to her own work. Now she could make the pictures. With India ink and brush, she made a few sketches as samples. (There was no use illustrating the whole story until she knew whether the editor liked it or not.) And the book was ready to submit.

To Eleanor's delight, Mrs. Hamilton was pleased with the story of *Little Pear* and accepted it at once. And the sample illustrations were satisfactory; she could go ahead with the others.

Happily the artist made the rest of the pictures—one

hundred and five of them in all! This was the goal she had been working toward. This was being an artist.

Little Pear was published in 1931. Its success pleased the author-illustrator immensely, for it meant not only that she could now make a living, but that as long as she could write stories, she would have books to illustrate. She could do the work she loved best.

20. *From Pole to Pole*

Silver Chief — O'Brien, 1933

IF YOU LOVE animals, undoubtedly you love dogs. If you love dogs, Silver Chief is probably one of your favorites among the dog heroes of fiction.

Silver Chief, Dog of the North, is a thrilling story of a wild dog, half-wolf and half-Husky, who came at last to know and love a man and who eventually saved that man's life. The story is so genuine that you feel, as you read it, as if it were actually happening. This is not at all strange because the man who wrote it knew what he was talking about; he had been through experiences such as those he wrote about, and many more. Moreover, Silver Chief was a real dog whom he himself had captured and tamed.

In the early 1930's Jack O'Brien, surveyor, prospector, writer, but most of all adventurer, was in northern Canada, working on a geographical survey and prospecting on the side. With the town of Churchill, on Hudson's Bay, as his base, he traversed the snow-covered land of the Arctic Circle, with no one for company except his sled dogs. Often he did not see a human being for many weeks at a time.

A lonely life and a hard life; danger was his constant companion. But danger was meat and drink to Jack O'Brien. From his early youth he had followed adventure around the world—in the army in Mexico, in the air corps during the first World War, with Admiral Byrd on the first Antarctic Expedition. Yes, for O'Brien the last twenty years had been just one succession of difficult and risky jobs, from the Antarctic to the Arctic.

Now, in the winter of 1932-33, O'Brien was off on another lonely adventure—a prospecting trip this time, in sub-zero temperature, in a land of ice and snow. With his sledge carefully loaded with provisions for a three-months' trip, and his dogs the best in that country (his life might depend on his dogs, he knew), Jack O'Brien set out.

As he traveled, occasionally he met an Indian or passed an Indian village. From these natives he heard strange rumors about a dog, a huge, beautiful animal who was as wild as a wolf, and as fierce. The Indians thought him a ghost; they called him Silver Chief.

The stories he heard of this phantom dog captured O'Brien's imagination. He loved dogs. And a dog who could do all the things the Indians attributed to this wild one of the northern woods must be a highly intelligent animal. He would like to catch him and tame him. But the Indians said this Silver Chief was too fast and too clever to be captured. Well, thought O'Brien as he traveled on north, that remained to be proved. First he would have to see the dog. . . . And there might not be such an animal, really. It might be just the Indians' imagination.

Weeks later, however, Jack O'Brien knew that the huge wild dog was not a figment of imagination. One moonlight night he saw him, and the beauty of the magnificent animal took his breath away. His earlier thought that it would be interesting to catch and tame such a highly intelligent creature became an obsession: he *must* have that dog!

For weeks Jack O'Brien tried in every way he knew to capture the beautiful, silvery-white dog. But, as the Indians had said, the animal was too smart to walk into ordinary traps; he could not be coaxed with food. At last, by means of a snare and harness to prevent injury, the big dog was caught. And then began the long, difficult struggle to tame him.

O'Brien knew dogs, especially the strong breed of Huskies. Not only had he worked with them in his years of prospecting and surveying in the Far North, but he had been in charge of one of the dog teams on the Byrd Expedition in the Antarctic. Now his experience stood him in good stead. With inexhaustible patience and unfailing kindness, he worked with his wild captive. Eventually he was rewarded by seeing the silver dog's fear and hate turn to love and loyalty and trust. It was a thrilling and deeply satisfying experience.

Back in Churchill in the spring, with Silver Chief an obedient and devoted pet by now, Jack O'Brien began to contemplate the possibility of writing down his experiences in taming the beautiful dog. Other dog lovers might be interested, too. Should he write a straight, factual account for adults—a magazine article, maybe? Or should he write it as a story for boys and girls?

The story idea won. O'Brien himself had always loved to read the animal and adventure books which are written for children. Now he would write one.

So the story of Silver Chief was begun, in the little town of Churchill, on Hudson's Bay. The dog hero O'Brien drew from life, from his now inseparable companion. The human hero he made into a Northwest "Mountie"; but the feelings and actions of Jim Thorne, Mounted Policeman, were those of Jack O'Brien, prospector and adventurer.

The book went swiftly and easily, like the writing of a diary, for O'Brien was telling of things he knew well. When it was finished, *Silver Chief, Dog of the North* was accepted immediately by John C. Winston Company and published in 1933.

At once it became popular with young readers all over the country. Silver Chief soon became mascot, hero, and friend to children in many lands.

Then girls and boys wanted to know more about Silver Chief. So Jack O'Brien wrote another book and then another, always drawing on his own experiences and observations for material. Thus he found his years of adventure and hardships an excellent source of exciting stories for boys and girls.

21. *Picture in Print*

The Good Master — Seredy, 1935

WHEN KATE, THE city child from Budapest, went to visit her cousin Jansci, who had lived all his life in the country on the plains of Hungary, things began to happen. Kate's visit changed life for Jansci from the moment of her arrival, and it also changed her own life— though she did not realize it at the time.

The Good Master is a delightful story of a madcap girl. But it is more than that: it is an authentic picture of life on the plains of Hungary, a picture painted in colors as bold and vivid as the costumes worn by the Hungarian peasants. And it was the work of an artist who had painted with brushes all her life but who had never before attempted to paint with words.

It was the morning of February 13, in 1934. To Kate Seredy it seemed that the depression was getting worse instead of better—though there were times, like today, when she thought her fortunes must have reached absolute zero and any change must be an improvement. Twelve years earlier she had arrived in

New York from her native Budapest, an unknown artist with no knowledge of English to help her in her attempts to find work. By the time she had mastered the language of her adopted country and convinced book publishers that she was an illustrator of real ability, the depression hit the publishing business, and she was again out of work. It was enough to discourage anyone.

But small, dark Kate Seredy was not discouraged. Something would turn up, she was sure. Today she was going to drive to New York to see an editor and show her some illustrations she had made, and perhaps something would come of that interview. Of course, her old Ford coupe had practically no radiator, and there was no money to have it fixed. Snow and ice covered the New Jersey country roads, and she had no chains. But *somehow* she would make that Ford cover the necessary miles and meet that editor in New York.

Hurriedly, Miss Seredy went around the huge, dilapidated mansion which she called home (she lived there because it was beautiful and because the rent was next to nothing) to see that everything would be all right in her absence. She fed the cats almost the last food in the house, filled the remains of the Ford's radiator with hot water, hoping that would satisfy the machine's thirst until she reached a garage, and started off.

The car had barely rattled out of the yard, however, when she was stopped by the sight of a coal black cat glaring at her from the snow-covered bushes by the side of the road.

Heavens! February 13, temperature 13 below, and

a black cat! What inauspicious omens for an interview on which so much depended!

But kindness quickly overpowered silly superstition. Regardless of its color, the poor cat must be cold and hungry. Kate Seredy jumped out of the car and returned to the house for the remaining scraps of food. When the strange cat was sheltered and fed, she made another start.

This time she reached the nearest town, five miles away. Almost obscured in a cloud of steam, the chainless, radiatorless Ford slid sidewise on the ice and came to a stop in front of the town's garage.

The garage man came out. He looked at the car. Then he gazed pityingly at its driver.

"Say, lady, you shouldn't be driving that car. The radiator—"

"Yes, I know," Miss Seredy admitted. "But I have to. I simply *have* to get into New York this morning."

"You ought to have chains anyway. It's dangerous, driving on these roads without chains."

"But I haven't any chains. And I haven't—" She stopped, but the garage man understood. Lots of the best people had no money these days.

"I've got an old pair of chains you can have," he offered, "if you'll bring them back tonight."

Thankfully Kate Seredy accepted the offer, and the strong hands of the mechanic soon had them in place.

Once more the artist started off. For a while everything went well. The steam from the radiator was not quite enough to blot out the road and the chains kept the old car on the highway.

Then there was an ominous *Wham!* followed by a continuous, *Clank, clank, clank!* What now? Had the rest of the radiator dropped out, or had she lost the carburetor?

Resignedly, Kate Seredy stopped the car and got out to see what the trouble was. One of the chains had broken and had wrapped itself around the wheel, defying all her efforts to get it loose.

She looked up and down the road. Not a house in sight, and not a single car. There was nothing to do but go on, in spite of the ear-splitting rattle.

At last she reached New York City and the offices of The Viking Press. Cold, hungry, dirty, and completely exhausted and tense from her long battle with the car, Kate Seredy tucked her portfolio of sketches under her arm and marched up to the office of May Massee, children's editor.

Miss Massee took one look at the artist's face and said, "Suppose we go out for a bite to eat. We can talk better over some hot tea."

Under the influence of the hot drink and the good food that went with it, Kate Seredy relaxed. With the stimulus of Miss Massee's interest and questions, she began to talk. She found herself telling of her long years of struggle to get work in New York and of her childhood in Hungary. Her long, thin hands gestured expressively as she poured out her problems and her dreams to this sympathetic, understanding listener.

Back in the office later, Miss Massee looked over the sketches.

"These are beautiful," she said. "You have a rare quality, Miss Seredy . . . I wish. . . . But there isn't a thing, not a thing in the office I can give you to illustrate, and nothing coming in that I know of."

Kate Seredy's spirits, which had been steadily rising since the first moment of her meeting with May Massee, took a sudden and sickening drop.

"Nothing?" she faltered. "I'd do *anything* . . ."

Miss Massee shook her head regretfully. "Not a thing. But why don't you write a book yourself and illustrate it?"

Kate Seredy laughed, a brave if rather forlorn laugh. "Why, I have never written anything. I wouldn't know how to go about it. I couldn't write a book."

May Massee looked at her appraisingly. "I think you could. Go home and try it. You may remember some things about Hungary—some childhood experiences that would make a good story. You just go home and write, and I'll publish it for Christmas."

When she reached her thirty-three-room house at Ramsey, New Jersey, Kate Seredy obediently sat down, pencil in hand, to write. The cats crowded around her. She petted them absently, her mind on her problem. Miss Massee had said she might remember things from her own childhood, so she turned her mind back to those long-ago days when she had been a child in Budapest. What stood out in her mind most clearly? Why, that was easy: those summers in the country.

Kate Seredy remembered vividly the first of those summers. Her father, an excellent and well-loved teacher of boys, had been invited to go to the country with a group of visiting artists and scientists to study peasant art and life. Kate's parents had decided that a few weeks in the country would be good for her and that she should accompany her father. Her protests that she did not want to go with a lot of old men to look at old things did no good. She went.

Never would Kate forget the evening they arrived in the small, remote village. Tired and sleepy and rebellious, the pale, skinny city child was immediately taken in hand by a motherly, rosy-cheeked peasant woman. This kind person tried to get her to drink foamy fresh milk "to put meat on her bones," but Kate preferred sausage and fresh bread, and scorned the warm milk. At bedtime she had been tucked into featherbeds; she could still recall how she had felt as she sank into those featherbeds—as if she were lost, sinking deeper and deeper into some fathomless pool.

Sitting in her big, cold house, surrounded by cats, thinking about those childhood experiences on the plains of her native land, Kate Seredy began to write. Almost without her volition, the pencil went on and on, telling the story of a spoiled city child suddenly dropped into the quiet, peaceful, wholesome life of Hungarian farmers—generous, honest people who worked hard and loved deeply. . . .

After three months of nearly constant writing, Kate Seredy woke up. Why, she had written almost enough for a book! It *was* enough. So she wrapped up the manuscript and sent it to May Massee at The Viking Press.

Three days later she delightedly received a contract. The book was accepted. She was to illustrate it and she could make as many pictures as she wished!

Again in a daze—of happiness this time—Kate Seredy turned artist and illustrated the book she had written without realizing it.

The Good Master was an immediate success. The depression was over for Kate Seredy. Something had indeed turned up—something she had never in her wildest dreams expected: the ability to write; though she always said that she didn't *write* the book at all—she merely gave a frame to the picture of Hungarian country life that many unknown peasants had painted for her years ago when she was a child.

22. The Loss That Was Not a Loss

Honk, the Moose — Stong, 1935

WHAT WOULD YOU do if you found a moose in your barn, or your garage? Yes, a moose: one of those huge animals whose antlers are so big they look like the branches of a tree; that outsize member of the deer family which is ordinarily found only in the wilds of the north woods.

Honk, the Moose is a hilarious tale of a moose that adopted a town. Once read, the story stays in the mind of the reader. But that is only fair, for it lingered in the mind of the author for fifteen years before he wrote it.

Early in the year of 1935, Philip Duffield Stong and his wife (both of them writers) were taking a vacation cruise in the Caribbean with some friends.

But Phil Stong had been a writer for so many years that he found it hard to keep away from his typewriter, even on a holiday. Moreover, the pleas of Dorothy Bryan (who had been responsible for his first juvenile book, *Farm Boy*) for another children's story kept ring-ing in his ears. By the time the boat headed north on the way back to New York, he was definitely restless.

"You know, Virginia," he said to his wife one day as they sat on the deck, watching the islands slip past, "I heard a story once that has been bothering me for years. A story about a town moose."

"A town moose!" repeated his wife. "I never heard of such a thing."

"That's just it," Phil Stong laughed. "It's a crazy idea. But one time, it was in 1920, I believe—" And he went on to tell Virginia Stong how he had heard the story of the town moose.

Stong had been teaching in Biwabik, Minnesota, at the time, and serving as athletic director. Late in November, he had gone to Ely, Minnesota, to play football with the Biwabik town team. *Br-rr!* How cold it was when they got there! The visiting team was glad enough to crowd into the warm lobby of the hotel and shiver at the thought of going out into the icy air for the game that afternoon.

While the men waited for lunch to be served, they compared notes about the coldest weather they had ever experienced. The tales got taller and taller, as each narrator tried to outdo the others.

Finally one chap said, "Aw, you fellows don't know what cold weather is. In our town it got so cold one winter a moose came into our livery stable to get warm."

A shout of laughter greeted that statement. But the

man did not smile. "That's a fact," he insisted. "The moose hung around all that winter. Sort of adopted us. We fed him hay."

Young Phil Stong chuckled at the idea of a moose becoming a town pet. And the older Phil Stong chuckled again as he told his wife about it, fifteen years later.

"Can you imagine it?" he finished. "And the fellow was dead serious. . . . We lost the game," he added regretfully. "Ely won, 23 to 13, I think it was."

"But, Phil," exclaimed Virginia, "why don't you write that story? It's priceless! Children would love it. A moose coming into a town and making himself at home. . . ." Her voice trailed off.

Phil Stong took it up, his eyes shining. "And some youngsters find him and they name him Honk and . . ." With growing enthusiasm, Stong planned his story.

At last he cried, "I'll do it, Virginia! I'll go and start right now."

So, in a tropical climate, Phil Stong began his story about a place where the thermometer dropped to forty degrees below zero. Sitting in front of two open portholes, with the electric fan going in an effort to keep from sweltering, he wrote about a winter that was so cold a moose came into town to get warm.

It was a rough trip back to New York. Most of the party suffered from seasickness. But Phil Stong sat at his typewriter day after day and pounded out the story of Honk, the Moose, and the trouble that was caused by his fondness for the warm livery stable and his insatiable appetite for hay.

Back home again, the book was interrupted while the Stongs settled themselves in a New York apartment. When writing was resumed, the story was soon finished and published in short order by Dodd, Mead and Company. Clever illustrations by Kurt Wiese pointed up the humor in the rollicking tale.

Honk, the Moose was popular from the start. It made Phil Stong a favorite author among children, as his *State Fair* and *Stranger's Return* had established his name among adult readers. So the story he heard the day his team lost to Ely brought Phil Stong both money and reputation. The lost game gave him a winning idea.

23. *The Book She Had to Write*

Shuttered Windows — Means, 1938

IF YOU LIVED in a country in which most of the population and most of the people in power belonged to a different race from your own, how would you feel? If you were looked upon as "different" and "inferior," what would that attitude do to you?

In a country which is predominantly white in population, life is not always easy for those whose skins are a different color. Yet all men are brothers under the skin. And with our country and the world growing smaller, as distances are shortened by rapid communication and transportation, it is becoming more and more important that we understand and appreciate our brothers of other races.

Books can do a lot to help this understanding. And *Shuttered Windows* is a good book to start with, for it is not only a sympathetic and accurate picture of the problems of a minority group, but it is also an absorbing story from the first page to the last.

It was autumn of 1935. Florence Crannell Means of

Denver was spending her last day at Mather School, in South Carolina. She hated to leave. How much she had enjoyed these weeks on the All-Negro campus! How different it had been from her expectations!

"Don't think," she had been warned before she came, "that these Negro girls of the Islands and the Carolina Lowlands will be friendly. You've written books about Mexican, American, Japanese, and Jewish children, and you've found them all easy to make friends with. But this time it will be different. Many Negroes resent white people, and these especially. You'll be sorry if you go."

Now Mrs. Means, busy with her packing and her final visits with teachers who had become friends, laughed as she remembered that dire prophecy. Sorry she had come! Why, it had been a wonderful experience. She had chosen this school in the first place because Mather's practice teaching school seemed a good place to get much of the material she wanted for the small books she had planned to write on little children of the Deep South. And she had not only found the material she wanted, but had made many friends among the teachers, and among the teen-age girls as well.

How good the girls had been to her! Every morning some one of them made her bed, someone put flowers in her room; every night someone turned her bed down. There had been grand hikes and parties. Yes, although at first they had been reserved and proud, these girls had come to be as friendly and lovable as any she had ever known. She was going to miss them.

The last day at Mather passed all too quickly. It was time for bed. Everything was ready for an early start next morning. But something bothered Mrs. Means. All day long, during the succession of visits from teachers, she had looked up at intervals to see disappointed young faces bob back out of sight. The girls were trying to get a chance to see her, and so far they had failed.

As soon as she realized this, Florence Means—without wasting a moment—went to the principal. "The girls want to say good-bye to me. Couldn't you let them come for a while, even though it is time for the evening bell?"

The principal smiled. "Why, yes. I think we could suspend the rules for once, since you are leaving so early in the morning."

Soon the girls began to gather in Mrs. Means' room, tall girls and short girls, in nighties, robes, and slippers —most of them with heads carefully wrapped so that the damp night air should not "take out the straight." In a few minutes the room was filled to overflowing.

But "good-bye" was the least of what the girls wanted to say. They wanted to talk. They wanted to talk about themselves to the woman whose sympathy and understanding had so impressed them. At once they began, prompting and correcting and interrupting each other, pouring out their hopes and fears, their immediate plans and their dreams for the future.

Until almost midnight the girls talked, and Mrs. Means listened and glowed with the knowledge of their trust and friendship.

At last Susan and Jessie Ree (two of the leaders among the older girls) exchanged glances. And brilliant, volatile Jessie Ree burst out, "Mis' Means, we wish you'd write a book about *us!* Just as if we were white girls! . . . And *leave the problem out.*"

Florence Crannell Means looked at the vivid face, and a mist came into her brown eyes. These splendid girls! Write about them? Why, she would love to. But . . . leave the problem out? She took off her glasses and wiped them thoughtfully. Before she could say anything, Susan began to speak—Susan, the tall, straight, independent, who could always be counted on for clear thinking. "Oh, Jessie Ree," she cried in her rich, vibrant voice, "nobody could write about us and leave the problem out!"

All around the room heads nodded. It was true. No one knew any better than they themselves that the problem could not be evaded. White girls could ignore the problem, but it was always staring Negro girls in the face.

Long after the room was empty and quiet, and the lights out, at last, Mrs. Means thought about the girls and what they had said. And the conviction grew upon her that she had to write that book.

Nearly two years passed, however, before Florence Means began to write the book which the Mather girls had requested. In the meantime, she had talked the idea over with her husband, as she did all her writing plans.

"I think you'd better drop the idea, Flossy," he advised. "It's a controversial subject. You might get some unpleasant repercussions."

Her editor was no more encouraging. "It's a bad subject for a book. I'm afraid it wouldn't sell."

In spite of all efforts to dissuade her, however, Mrs. Means found that she simply could not drop the idea. She *had* to write that book.

Finally, in July, 1937, she began it. At first it worried her that she did not know the sea islands of South Carolina. A few weeks' residence, she knew, is not enough to enable one to write convincingly about a place. But she soon saw that if her heroine did not know the vicinity either, that did not matter. The setting and the people could be pictured through the eyes of a new-comer. So Harriet (who was inspired by Susan at Mather) became a girl brought up in Chicago who was going to the home of her people in South Carolina.

Soon Harriet and all the other characters came alive as Mrs. Means wrote in her spruce tree study (a sturdy table under a circle of spruces on the hillside behind the Means' summer cabin in the mountains near Denver). All summer long she worked and on into the fall, after the family had moved back into Denver for the winter.

When she was about halfway through the book, a title suddenly occurred to her. She remembered those windowless cabins that were so common on the islands: no glass, merely shutters which, when open, let in the bitter cold and rain in the winter, and—closed—shut out the light. Was not that the way it was with so many of Harriet's race? If they were friendly and free with white people, they laid themselves open to coldness and unkindness; if they kept to themselves, they had comparatively little chance for learning and advancement. Yes, *Shuttered Windows* was the title for her book.

When the first draft of *Shuttered Windows* was completed, Florence Means sent a copy to the teachers at Mather School, to be read to the girls and checked for accuracy of detail and interpretation. Almost unanimously the Mather people approved. Her husband (still doubtful about the wisdom of publishing it), her parents, and her daughter all read the manuscript and pronounced it good. Even the editor who had been discouraging when Mrs. Means first suggested the idea, decided it was too good a book to pass up. So, in 1938, *Shuttered Windows* was published, and the book she simply *had* to write, against the advice of family and editor, has come to be considered one of the best of the many good books written by Florence Crannell Means.

24. Lucky Lay-off

Blue Willow — Gates, 1940

BLUE WILLOW IS the absorbing story of a little girl whose entire life has been spent moving over the countryside from place to place, as her father finds a few weeks' work in one seasonal job after another. All this time she has longed for a real home—any place with four walls where they could stay on for months (maybe a year, even!) and have a chance to make some friends like other children. She wants a home so very much that in order to get it she is willing to give up the only beautiful thing she has ever possessed, her blue willow plate.

This moving story of the children of migratory workers is one of those rare and valuable books which give boys and girls a little insight into the lives of less fortunate children. Yet the author might never have discovered that she could write if the Fresno County Library had not run short of funds.

In 1936 Doris Gates was a children's librarian in Fresno County, California. All her life she had loved

books, especially books for boys and girls. Even if
there had been time for it, however, she had never
thought of writing herself. She kept busy with her
library work and spent her spare time trout-fishing and
horseback riding.

Then one day Miss Gates received a most unwelcome
notice. For lack of sufficient funds to keep it open full
time, the library would be closed one day a week.

"Isn't that annoying?" she cried to her family when
she broke the news to them at dinner. "It will be a day
wasted every week."

Her father smiled. "Oh, it isn't as bad as all that,
Dorie. You can find plenty to occupy your time."

"But it has to be something useful," Doris answered.
"Oh, it's simply maddening, Dad! Just as I'm getting
started on my career, to have to waste a whole day
every week. What am I going to *do* with that time?"

"Why, rest, of course," answered her mother
promptly. "You work hard enough the other days,
Doris. I guess you can take a day off once a week without feeling guilty about it."

Doris shook her head. "No, Mother, I've got to find
something to do. I've got to make that spare day
count."

Some weeks later it occurred to her that she might
try writing. She had always been considered a good
letter writer. Maybe she could write books—books for
children, of course, since they were her main interest.
It would not hurt to try.

Accordingly, every Wednesday, while the library

was closed, Doris Gates sat at her typewriter, trying to write. For a year everything she wrote went into the waste basket. But eventually she began to improve. The second year of Wednesday writing produced a book which was published in 1938 under the title of *Sarah's Idea*.

No sooner was her first book finished than Doris found herself thinking about another book. This time it was a dangerous subject she wanted to tackle: the very ticklish topic of migratory workers.

As head of the children's department of the Fresno County Free Library, she had served the migratory workers of the San Joaquin Valley. She had seen the children of these families who travel around the country, picking cotton near Fresno in the summer, moving on to another section when grapes were ripe, going south in the winter to pick oranges near Los Angeles, and lettuce in the Imperial Valley— Yes, Doris Gates had seen plenty of those underprivileged youngsters who have never known a real home, who have never owned a book and seldom have a chance even to read one. Some of the children were sensitive and intelligent and beauty-hungry, but what chance did they have? How could they learn anything, how could they ever get anywhere, when their lives were just one long succession of brief camps in crowded, unappetizing places— always in the most undesirable section of town? Surely the story of one of those children would be interesting to other more fortunate girls and boys. And she would write it.

Immediately Doris Gates set about learning more about such children. She told stories in migratory schools; she secured a job in a cotton field where she had a chance to get acquainted with the parents; she visited some of the families with a social worker; and she visited migrant camps alone and talked with the people. Always she was given a friendly reception, and her sympathy grew for these unfortunate wanderers who were looked down on by settled, substantial townsfolk.

Although she did not talk about what she was doing, word got around among her friends that Doris Gates was writing about the migrants, and she became the recipient of much unsolicited advice.

"Doris, surely you're not going to write about a controversial subject like the Oakies! Why, everyone in town will be down on you."

"Why waste your time on a book that won't sell? No editor would touch a book on a subject like that . . . . And even if you got it published, people wouldn't buy it for their children."

"Children won't be interested in what happens to a little 'Oakie.' You've seen for yourself, Doris, how the town children treat those kids from the migrant camps. Stick to nice, clean stories about ordinary youngsters."

But Doris Gates paid little attention. Oh, she knew her well-meaning friends were right. She would probably never get this book published. But maybe if she soft-pedaled the problem . . . She found herself pulling her punches and glossing over the hard facts of the problem.

When *Blue Willow* was finished, Miss Gates sent it to The Viking Press. Soon she received a letter from the children's editor. To the author's complete amazement, far from objecting to publishing a book on the controversial subject of migratory workers, the editor liked it but felt that the presentation could be better.

That was all Doris needed. She sat down at her typewriter and rewrote *Blue Willow*, and this time she pulled no punches. Nothing was glossed over, nothing soft-pedaled. And this time, when the book was finished, The Viking Press accepted it immediately and published it in 1940.

Contrary to her friends' dire predictions, Doris Gates found that not only did a publisher accept her book, but children read it and liked it. In fact, it soon became one of the most popular books published in recent years.

Thus it was that the enforced vacation, which seemed at the time so annoying and frustrating, turned out to be a blessing in disguise, for it gave Doris Gates a chance to discover that she could write. Now, besides helping children to discover the world of books, she could add her own contribution to the list of well-loved books for boys and girls.

25. Two-Country Author

Lassie Come-Home — Knight, 1940

THE LOVE OF a boy for a dog, and the loyalty of the dog to that boy: There is no more appealing book theme for anyone who has ever had a dog, or loved a dog, or wanted one—and who has not?

Lassie Come-Home is one of the most enthralling dog stories ever written. The saga of Lassie's struggle, against fearful odds, to keep her habitual appointment with the boy who loved her is absorbing and exciting from the first page to the last. It is a story that will undoubtedly be read and loved as long as there are young people to read it.

Some books grow from a certain character or a single incident with its specific background, and are written for a definite audience. But *Lassie Come-Home*, like its author, was drawn from two countries. Not only that, it was at first neither a short story nor a book, but became each of those in turn. In addition, it was really written for adults, and became a children's book almost by accident.

In the 1930's, Eric Knight was enjoying life on his farm in Pleasant Valley, Pennsylvania. Though he had been writing ever since his arrival in America at the age of fifteen, most of his time in recent years had been occupied by newspaper work, service in the British Army during World War I, and writing for the movies in Hollywood, leaving little leisure for the novels and stories he liked best to do. Now at last he had given up other work and intended to make writing a full-time career.

This was the life he loved: congenial companionship —his wife Jere (also a writer), his daughter Betty, plenty of friends dropping in from time to time; his beloved collies and horses; room to breathe; space for the things he liked to do—riding, hunting, farming; and leisure for writing whatever he wanted to write, not what some editor or producer told him to. Yes, this was a good life.

One day in 1938 Eric Knight was casting around in his mind for a story idea. His book, *The Flying Yorkshireman*, had just been published and was a Book-of-the-Month selection. Now he wanted to start something else.

As he rode over the farm or walked through the woods with his collies at his heels, he kept searching for a subject to write about.

One day the Knights drove to the city on business. As usual, the collie Toots (originally named Lassie) accompanied them in the car. When Eric Knight finally parked at the intersection of a busy street, he left the dog in the locked car with a window open sufficiently for ventilation but not enough to allow the dog to get out and wander off—he thought.

Their errands took longer than they expected. On the way back to the car, the Knights walked rapidly. Toots would be anxious to get out; she had been caged in far too long.

As they came in sight of the automobile, they stopped and stared. A collie sat alertly on the running board. It looked like Toots! But how had she managed to get out of the car?

A stranger stood on the sidewalk near by. "That your dog?" he asked as they approached.

"Why, yes," Knight answered, trying the car door. "But I can't understand how she got out. That window is nearly closed, and the door is still locked."

The man laughed. "She's some dog, all right. She wriggled and worked till she managed to get through that window. Once I thought she was stuck for sure, but she made it somehow. Wonderful dog! I've tried for half an hour to coax her away from the car, but she wouldn't budge. No, sir. She's your dog, mister, and she won't go to anyone else."

As Eric Knight and his wife drove toward Springhouse Farm, they talked about the cleverness and loyalty of their dog.

"Remember the time we thought she was lost?" asked Jere.

Eric Knight nodded. He would not soon forget it. They had been riding a long distance from home that day, and Toots had chased a rabbit into the woods. At first they thought nothing of it. She would come back. But when hours passed and she did not show up, they began to search for her.

It was no use. Toots was lost. She did not answer or come at their call. At last, heavy-hearted, her owners started home. How they would miss the devoted collie! Although they owned several other dogs, none could take the place of Toots, who had been with them so long and had made such a big place for herself in their hearts. They would advertise for her, of course, but it was sure to be useless. It was too much to hope that an honest person would find the handsome, pure-bred collie and return her. And she was too far from home to be able to find her way back unaided.

The days that followed were dreary ones at Springhouse Farm. Everybody missed Toots—even the other dogs. And then—it wasn't possible, but it happened—Toots came back! She had found her way home, alone, through many miles of strange country! She was a one-man dog, a come-home dog. Nothing could keep her from the man she loved.

There had been other incidents since which proved that Toots' loyalty to her master was the strongest force in her life.

And now, after learning that Toots had again done the impossible in crawling out through the nearly closed car window, Eric Knight said to his wife, "I believe that dog could do anything and go anywhere if she felt she had to."

"If she felt she must find you," added Jere.

As the days passed, Eric Knight found himself thinking more and more of Toots and her blind, unquestioning devotion. A come-home dog she was. Well, why not write a story about a come-home dog? A collie, of course. And naturally, since the Yorkshire of his boyhood was the home of some of the finest collies in the world, the story should be set in Yorkshire, England.

So *Lassie Come-Home* was written and sent to Knight's literary agent in New York.

"This is a swell story," wrote his agent in a few days. "I think the *Post* will like it. But it is too long for a short story. Can't you cut it?"

So the author took out all the passages he felt could be deleted, and the story was accepted and published in *The Saturday Evening Post* of December 17, 1938.

Sometime later Knight was talking to his friend, Jack Fraser of John C. Winston Company.

"I read that story of yours in the *Post*, about Lassie," he said. "It's a great story. Children would love it."

Knight nodded. "My daughter Betty liked it. She kept wanting me to make it longer. Then my agent persuaded me to shorten it! You can't please everyone."

"Well, why don't you make it longer and let me publish it as a book for children?"

It was a splendid idea. And as easily done as said; for all that Eric Knight had to do was to put back in the passages he had taken out before, and the book was ready for the press!

Lassie Come-Home was published as a book in 1940. At once children proved that Jack Fraser was right, for it soon became one of the favorite books of boys and girls the country over, and has remained so ever since.

26. The Blessing of the Hurricane

Call It Courage — Sperry, 1940

HAVE YOU EVER been called a coward? Have you ever been afraid of anything? Have you ever felt you had to overcome some special fear and prove to yourself that you are not a coward?

Then you can understand how Mafatu, the Polynesian boy, felt about his fear of the sea. You can see why he had to go away from his island—his home—and conquer the fear that had followed him all his life.

Call It Courage is an inspiring story for both the brave and the timid. It is a story you will read and re-read, and like better with each reading. It grew from an old legend and was inspired by something that happened while the author was living in the South Seas.

In 1939, on his thirty-acre farm in Connecticut, Armstrong Sperry, author-illustrator, had just finished his seventh book for children and was wondering what to write next. As had happened so often when he was casting about for a subject for a book, his thoughts went back to the two years he had spent in the South Seas.

What a wonderful experience that had been, sailing to the South Seas on a copra schooner, wandering among the least-known islands of the Pacific, living with the hospitable, child-like natives who accepted him without question as a friend. What a carefree, idyllic existence it had been, especially on the island of Bora Bora. Until the hurricane. . . . Always, in thinking of those years in the South Seas, Sperry's mind went back to the hurricane and what that disaster had accomplished.

He had been living on the island of Bora Bora, as a guest of the chief, Opu Nui. Life in that beautiful spot was perfect. There was no hunger. Everyone had plenty to eat, for there were always breadfruit and bananas for the picking, and fish for the catching. The people made their own clothes of tapa bark. They built their own houses of bamboo. Everyone worked leisurely, lighthearted and happy, harvesting copra and vanilla beans for the schooners which would come to carry them away. In the evenings they sat around their fires, singing the old songs of their people and telling the traditional stories of how their ancestors had crossed the ocean in sailing canoes before the dawn of history. No one on the island ever thought of locking doors, for no one owned anything that others could not have, themselves, if they wanted to. Yes, Bora Bora was a veritable Garden of Eden.

But one day a schooner brought big news. A blight had struck the vanilla bean on all the other islands. Only Bora Bora had escaped this blight; their vanilla beans were still perfect, and since vanilla would now be scarce, their beans would bring higher prices—much higher prices.

At first the news meant nothing to the happy Polynesians. What was money? They did not need it. They had everything they needed. But soon merchants and shopkeepers began to arrive at Bora Bora. They showed the natives what money would buy: store clothes instead of tapa cloth garments; frame bungalows in place of bamboo huts; cars to ride in, jewelry, ornaments, motion-picture shows.

Sperry felt as if he had a front seat for a tragi-comic play as he watched the change which came over the simple, lovable Polynesians when they realized that money—the money their vanilla beans brought—could buy all these things. The people were no longer happy to live simply, as they had before. Now they must have frame houses and fine clothes; they must have everything their neighbors had—and more. Soon quarrels broke out, and robbery and fighting and killing. Bora Bora was no longer an ideal place to live.

One day Sperry said to his friend, the chief, "It's time I was leaving; there are other islands I want to visit."

Opu Nui looked at his guest and shook his head sadly. "That is not the reason you are going, my friend. You do not like what is happening here on Bora Bora. That is why you wish to go away."

Sperry could not deny it. "Your people are different since all this money came to the island."

"Yes," agreed the chief. "My people are not the same. They are forgetting the old ways. No longer do they gather around the fires in the evening and sing the old songs and tell the old stories. No one hunts the wild pig today or spears the octopus or stabs the shark."

"They do not need to now," Sperry pointed out. "All they have to do is go to the store and buy what they want."

"It is not good, this that is happening," said Opu Nui, shaking his head. "We were a great people once. We had great courage. Our people crossed this ocean in sailing canoes when the world was young. Could any of the people of Bora Bora today do that? Do they have courage?"

Sperry could not answer that. He merely said again that he must leave soon—on the next schooner, probably.

But the old chief begged him to wait. "It is almost the season of storms," he said. "Wait until they are over. February is the time of hurricanes. After that it will be safe to go."

So Sperry waited. And he would always be glad he did.

Toward the end of February a hurricane struck— such a hurricane as Bora Bora had not seen in many years. Terrific winds and tremendous waves battered the island, and the people retreated to the mountain slopes for safety. When the storm was over at last and the people could return to their homes, what a sight greeted their eyes! All of their houses, both bamboo and frame, had been swept away. The trees were stripped bare of both leaves and fruit. Nothing was left on the naked island, neither homes nor food nor crops nor money.

The people of Bora Bora were overwhelmed with despair—all but Opu Nui. He gathered his people around him and talked to them. He reminded them of the courage of their forefathers, of the valor that was theirs by inheritance. He persuaded them to sing the old songs and chant the traditional stories. Sperry watched and listened, fascinated. Could the valiant old chief reawaken courage and hope in his people?

He could and he did. Before long the Polynesians of Bora Bora were rebuilding their ruined lives, using crude tools reminiscent of the Stone Age. The task required great ingenuity, for they had little to work with. But they rose to the occasion manfully. By the time medical supplies and implements arrived from Tahiti, such things were not needed. The people of Bora Bora had rebuilt their houses. They had proved that they were worthy descendants of the early Polynesians who had been so daring. Sperry had never forgotten the thrill it had given him to watch their reawakening courage.

Now, years later, as he was trying to decide on a subject for another book, Armstrong Sperry went back again to that matter of courage. He remembered an old legend he had heard in the South Seas of a boy who had gone away from his home to prove his courage to himself so that he could prove it to others. Why not write a book about such a boy? A boy who was afraid, but who set out to conquer his fear. The only true courage is that which knows fear; surely that was a worth while theme for a story. Perhaps it was too adult an idea for a children's book, but he would try it and see.

Accordingly, *Call It Courage* was written and illustrated by the author. Published by The Macmillan Company, in 1940, it was immediately popular with boys and girls, and the following year was awarded the Newbery Medal as the most outstanding book during the year of its publication.

Thus the hurricane which struck Bora Bora years ago proved to be a blessing by awakening the people of the island to their heritage of courage. And it also proved a blessing to the young artist who was visiting there at the time, for it helped him to write a book which will be an inspiration to American children for years to come.

27. Alternate Ambition

My Friend Flicka — O'Hara, 1941

Although he could ride any horse on the ranch, Ken wanted a horse of his own. He wanted a colt to gentle, to raise, to love. And of all the thoroughbred colts, his choice was the one his father considered not worth raising.

My Friend Flicka is more than an appealing story of a boy's love for a horse. It is an interesting study of the growth and development of an irresponsible, impractical boy. The book became a best-seller and embarked its author upon a career as novelist—but it was not the career she had chosen for herself.

In 1939 Mary O'Hara Sture-Vasa, wife of a Wyoming rancher, felt that she was on the threshold of success in her chosen field of music composition. Quite a few of her piano compositions had been published, under the name of Mary O'Hara, since she had come to the ranch to live. Some of these days she would write some really worth while music, and then the dream of her life would be fulfilled.

ALTERNATE AMBITION   143

But music and the work on the ranch (helping her husband with the horses, running a dairy, etc.) were not enough to satisfy her. She wanted to write, too. Perhaps it was because she had written for so many years; she had really made a name for herself in Hollywood as a scenario writer before she came to Wyoming. Writing had become a habit.

But writing did not come easy. Unlike music, which was a pleasure, writing was hard work.

One summer day Mary O'Hara was working on a dramatic story. As usual, each page cost her a struggle. Characters and scenes became increasingly difficult to handle.

At last she threw down the manuscript in disgust.

What was wrong, she wondered, looking out over the vast, lonely grandeur of the Wyoming landscape. Writing should not be as hard as that. Surely *good* writing—a really fine story—should flow more easily.

Perhaps that was the trouble. Perhaps she was telling the wrong story. . . .

Mary O'Hara thought about that. She remembered the sort of story she often told friends, a simple little tale about an animal. That kind of thing always seemed to go over well; maybe that was what she should write, instead of this dramatic stuff which gave her so much trouble.

The word "animal" naturally brought horses to mind. (One could not live on a ranch like this, with a husband who raised thoroughbred horses, without thinking in terms of colts and yearlings, fillies and geldings.) How about a story of a colt—perhaps a yearling with a wild strain which might be expected to cause trouble? She began to think over the colts they had raised.

Soon a little filly—a composite of several horses she had known—became a real character in her mind. A favorite word of her Swedish-American husband came back to her, and the filly was named "Flicka." Mary O'Hara snatched a pencil and began to make notes.

But the colt should have an owner. And that owner ought to be a boy. Now what kind of a boy. . . .

Gradually a boy took shape in her imagination, a dreamy, impractical, irresponsible youngster. Mary O'Hara's pencil raced across the pages, bringing the boy to life.

Before she realized it, the author had dropped her dramatic story entirely and was absorbed in jotting down bits that occurred to her about the boy Ken and his filly, Flicka. Soon it dawned on her that, instead of making notes, she was writing a story, and it was flowing as easily and smoothly as she had wanted it to. This writing was not work. It was fun!

In a few days *My Friend Flicka*, a short story of some six thousand words, was finished. Mary O'Hara sent it to *Story* magazine, and it was accepted and published.

Then the editor of *Story* suggested that *My Friend Flicka* might be made into a novel and put the author in touch with J. B. Lippincott Company.

Mary O'Hara worked for six months developing her short story about Ken and his filly into a novel. As with the original draft, the writing went easily and naturally. To her delight Mary O'Hara learned that when she had a good story to tell writing was no longer a terrible struggle.

My Friend Flicka was published in 1941, successful from the start. Soon it became a best-seller. Another book about Ken and his horse was demanded, and then another. So Mary O'Hara, who dreamed of making a name as a composer of music, carved for herself instead a career as an author.

28. *Returned with Interest*

Paddle-to-the-Sea — Holling, 1941

Do YOU LIKE to travel by water? Do you sometimes wish you could get into a little boat and go on and on, wherever the current would take you?

Paddle-to-the-Sea is the story of a tiny wooden Indian in a canoe, who drifted with the currents of the Great Lakes all the way from Lake Superior to the Atlantic Ocean. It is fun to follow his adventures, and it is educational as well, for you learn a lot about geography in tracing Paddle's long voyage.

This book was the work of a man who knew the waters and the shores he wrote about as well as the Indians of earlier years knew them; and Paddle himself came into being because of a generous and friendly act.

In the autumn of 1938, Holling Clancy Holling, author-illustrator, and his wife (also an artist) were on their way West in their studio-trailer. This was one of the ways the Hollings liked to travel when getting material for books. They could go where they wanted to go as fast or as slowly as they liked. They could stop and camp, and study and paint; they could pack up and be on the road again when other scenes beckoned. The trailer was a perfect traveling studio for these artist-writers.

Now they were on their way to the headwaters of the Missouri River, because Holling had promised Lovell Thompson, of Houghton Mifflin Company, that he would write a story about a river.

As the Hollings traveled toward Lake Superior, through Wisconsin, they talked about the Great Lakes and the fun they had had in that country. In previous years they had camped all around the Lakes on long canoe trips together, and Holling had spent two summers, during his high school days, working on Great Lakes freighters. Thus the Lakes were familiar territory to them.

One morning Holling pointed beyond pine-clad bluffs to where dark blue water met an endless sky.

"This country is big," he said. "I had almost forgotten how vast and wonderful it is."

Lucille laughed. "How could you 'almost forget' the greatest lakes in the world?"

"Think of it," continued Holling. "Here is a group of giant lakes with thousands of miles of waterway running entirely through them!" Then he stopped. An idea had struck him.

"Lucille!" he cried. "A *river* in the *Lakes!* That's what my new book will be: not a story about a lonely, thin river, but a fat, wide river in the Great Lakes!"

His wife thought a moment. "A *river* in the *Lakes—*

that's a good idea, Holling. But how will you do it? What will your story be?"

The author shook his head. "I don't know—yet."

A week or so later he found the answer—or thought he did. The Hollings were on a fishing boat on Lake Superior. Idly watching green water curling away from the bows, Holling saw a chip of wood dancing on the waves. It seemed to be tossed aimlessly to and fro; but he knew, from his knowledge of the currents in Lake Superior, that sooner or later that chip would be carried on through the Sault Sainte Marie into another lake, and then into another, and another.

"That's it!" he exclaimed. "A chip floats along the river in the Lakes, clear to the sea!"

A few weeks later, however, Holling's idea changed again. The travelers were now in Ontario, Canada, near Fort William. They met an Indian woman, a Chippewa, selling birchbark baskets or "makaks."

The Hollings looked at the baskets. They were well-made, but the decorations scraped on the bark were not Indian designs. They were badly drawn pictures copied from magazines: flower pots, sunbonnet babies, roses— The Hollings shuddered.

"Why don't you use the old-time Chippewa designs?" Lucille asked the woman. "They are beautiful."

The Indian shrugged. "My gran'mother, she make old Chippewa designs," she said. "But I not know them now. I have forgotten."

The Hollings turned away, saddened. What a shame that the beautiful old Indian designs should be forgotten by the very tribes that were once so expert in carving and painting them. Such things should be preserved from generation to generation.

When they reached the studio-trailer, the Hollings began to sketch from memory some patterns of Chippewa and Cree designs. They had traveled and camped among many tribes and for years had studied about Indians—their history, how they lived, their arts and crafts.

"Yes," said Holling, looking over their sketches, "these have the feel of the old symbols. Now let's make them up into real Chippewa-style patterns and take them to that makak-maker."

So the two artists set to work, gathering squares of birchbark from dead trees along a river. With sharp knives they cut bark silhouettes of their designs. With these flat, cardboard-like patterns laid on the side of a bark basket, the Indian woman could trace around them with a sharp-pointed bone, and scrape the bark inside these outlines; then the scraped areas would finally show up on the orange-brown "tree-side" of the basket as dark thunderbirds, underwater monsters, and leaf-and-plant designs.

The next morning the Hollings returned to the place where the Indian woman was trying to sell her baskets. Holling held out the design patterns.

"We made these for you," he said.

The Indian looked at the patterns in astonishment. "Chippewa!" she cried. "Like my gran'mother used to make! Now I remember. Now I remember the old designs!"

The Chippewa woman was so pleased to have the patterns of her tribe—authentic designs that had been forgotten in her family—that she loaded the Hollings with gifts—woven baskets, bark makaks, and crude carvings.

It was her final gift that Holling looked at curiously: a small carving of a kneeling Indian with a drawn bow.

"Who made this?" he asked.

"A young friend," answered the Indian, pleased with his pleasure. "A Chippewa boy."

"A boy made this?" Holling was surprised that such a delicate carving could have been made by young hands. "How old is the boy?"

"Eleven summers," was the answer.

As the Hollings carried the Indian woman's gifts back to their trailer, Holling's thoughts were busy. An eleven-year-old boy had carved a kneeling Indian with a drawn bow. Then why couldn't such a boy carve an Indian kneeling in a canoe? A canoe could float like a chip through the river in the lakes and travel clear to the sea! That would be the central figure for his story. . . .

So the idea of Paddle, carved by an Indian boy, began to develop. Later that fall, while the Hollings were camped in Bryce Canyon, Utah, Holling suddenly thought of having the boy carve on the bottom of the canoe, "I am Paddle-to-the-Sea," as an Indian would

say, "I am *paddling* to the sea." And there was his title:
Paddle-to-the-Sea.

Months of work followed. Weeks of study to
assemble and organize his material, to verify his facts.
Weeks of patient work on the illustrations, with water
color, pencil and pen. More weeks of patient work,
revising and cutting to make each page comprehensive
yet concise. And at last *Paddle-to-the-Sea* was finished
and off to the publishers.

The book was published in 1941, by Houghton
Mifflin Company. At once it became popular with
readers, who loved to follow Paddle's adventures on the
river in the Great Lakes. And it further established the
name of Holling Clancy Holling as a man who could
make beautiful, interesting, and worth-while books for
boys and girls. So the Hollings' investment in friendship
(in helping the Chippewa woman to remember the old-
time designs of her tribe) was returned with interest.

29. Uncorked Memories

The Moffats — Estes, 1941

DID YOU EVER look at the world upside down from between your legs or standing on your head? Did you ever look at the sky through a piece of colored glass? Did you ever try to scare someone on Hallowe'en?

Most people can remember doing things like that as children. That is probably what makes *The Moffats* so real to readers—the recollections and sensations and wonderings of early childhood which the story brings to mind.

It is no wonder that the Moffat books have the effect of reviving forgotten experiences and feelings, because they were written out of the memories and wonderings of the author's own childhood.

In the late 1930's, Eleanor Estes, children's librarian in a New York City public library, was still saying to herself, as she had done for years and years, "Some day I'm going to write."

From the time she was eleven she had intended to be a writer when she grew up. But she became a librarian instead, and was too busy, she felt, to write. Then she married, and became busier than ever, with housework added to her librarian duties. There just never seemed to be time to sit down and write.

So the years passed; but instead of diminishing, her desire to write grew stronger. Eleanor Estes found herself thinking more often of childhood sensations and emotions that she wanted to put down on paper. She found some of the silly wonderings of her little-girl years bothering her: What would happen if, on a one-track trolley line, the motorman disregarded a red light and went ahead anyway? What would happen if a child who was feeling guilty about some small misdemeanor met a policeman who was obviously looking for a criminal? What would happen if——? All her life her vivid imagination had been posing such questions to her mind. Some day, when she had time, she was going to write about things like that; she was going to write books for children.

But "some day" showed no signs of ever coming. Life was always busy, always full of responsibilities. There was never time to write.

One day, which was just as crowded as every other day, Eleanor Estes suddenly said to herself, "If I'm ever going to be a writer, I'd better start. I'd better get those books written." And she sat down with a pencil and paper.

Where should she begin? Well, why not start with that fascinating sensation she remembered so clearly, of looking at the world upside down? And she began to write.

Once started, her pencil kept on going. Once un-corked, the memories came rushing, begging to be put on paper. Naturally, since Mrs. Estes herself had been a child in a small New England town, the boys and girls she wrote about lived in just such a town. Since she had been one of several children in a poor family, the characters in her story belonged to such a family. Things she remembered, things she had observed, things she had wondered about, all got into the story, interwoven and interchanged until she could scarcely tell the difference between what she really remembered and what she had imagined.

But all authors must have an audience. After she had written a number of chapters, Eleanor Estes showed them to her husband, the reference librarian of Brook-lyn College.

Rice Estes took the handwritten manuscript and began to read.

Eleanor watched her husband's face anxiously. She had great respect for his opinions. Even if he didn't like it, though, even if no one liked it, she would go on. She had to write *The Moffats*.

Soon Rice Estes smiled. Then he chuckled. At last he broke into a hearty laugh. "This is *good!*" he ex-claimed. "It has humor and it has soul."

The young writer's face glowed. Her husband was an appreciative audience.

For two years Eleanor Estes wrote in whatever time she could spare from her other duties. Her book was finally finished and sent to a publisher.

Harcourt Brace accepted *The Moffats* immediately. And then came the question of an illustrator. Did the author have any suggestions?

Yes, she did. Mrs. Estes wanted Louis Slobodkin, the sculptor, to illustrate her book. She had met him a couple of years before, when she and her husband were on their summer vacation at Cape Ann, on the New England coast. She had long admired Slobodkin's work, and now she found that she liked his ideas about book illustration. (Although he had never yet tried illustrating, he had definite convictions about it.) Yes, Louis Slobodkin was the man Eleanor Estes wanted to do the pictures for her book.

When he was approached with the suggestion, Slobodkin agreed immediately, though privately he was considerably afraid that he would not be able to put into practice his fine-sounding theories about illustrating. To his relief, however, and to the joy of the author and the publisher, he was as successful at book illustration as at sculpture.

Immediately upon its publication in 1941, *The Moffats* found an enthusiastic audience among young readers. It became so popular that Eleanor Estes had to write another book about the Moffat family . . . and then another.

So it was that Eleanor Estes, librarian, finally fulfilled her childhood ambition, simply by sitting down with a pencil in her hand and uncorking her memories and wonderings.

PART FOUR

A Long Time Ago

30. *Persistent Vision*

Downright Dencey — Snedeker, 1927

DOWNRIGHT DENCEY HAS been a favorite with young readers for more than twenty years. The steadfastness and courage of the little Quaker girl and her persistence in accomplishing her purpose inspire devotion and admiration in readers, as they did in her friends of the story.

Dencey's persistence did not begin with her resolve to teach the outcast, Jetsam, to read. Long before a word had been written about her, she demonstrated conclusively the strength of her character, for from the time she first appeared in her author's mind, she directed and dominated the writing of her story.

By 1925 Caroline Dale Snedeker, wife of the Episcopalian minister at Hempstead, Long Island, was an established writer for young readers. *The Spartan, Perilous Seat* and other books were enjoying good sales and nice reviews.

In the summer of 1925, the Snedekers made their first trip to Nantucket, the little island off the coast of

Massachusetts. Soon after landing in the quaint old Quaker settlement, Mrs. Snedeker asked a resident to tell her a good place to eat lunch.

"Go up Fair Street to Darling and stop at Mrs. Folger's," she was told.

As she set out, alone, to find Mrs. Folger's, Caroline Snedeker mused on the charm of the street names on this island. Fair Street and Darling. . . .

And then she was in Fair Street, and all thought of lovely names left her. She scarcely saw the quaint gray Quaker houses which lined the street, or the low white fences, or the beautiful bright little gardens. Even the Meeting House, midway of the street, which she had looked forward to seeing, was merely a blur. For Caroline Dale Snedeker was seeing something else—or rather she was *feeling* something so strongly she could not see: she felt that here in this street something waited for her—something for a book.

The strange feeling persisted throughout the day. By the time another day had passed, Mrs. Snedeker knew that the "something" which Fair Street of Nantucket held for her was a little Quaker girl of an earlier day; a steadfast, downright Quaker who would hold to her convictions through punishment and persecution. She must know that girl better.

Wherever Mrs. Snedeker went in the days that followed, the Quaker child of early Nantucket went with her in her mind. Soon the writer began to read Nantucket history and records, to learn the background and heritage of the child. She talked with her friend, Mary

Starbuck, lifelong resident of Nantucket and a descendant of the first settlers there. Before long the little Quaker and her life and her home were as real to Mrs. Snedeker as any of the living people of the island. She felt she must write about her.

But she knew she could not. Nantucket and its history belonged to her friend Mary Starbuck, who was also a writer. She could not take something that belonged to another. Well, no matter. The child in her mind was a part of Nantucket and she would remain behind when they left the island.

When the Snedekers' Nantucket visit was over, however, the girl of the vision would not be left behind. She followed them back to Long Island. Such persistence!

"What shall I do?" cried Caroline Snedeker to her husband.

Her husband smiled kindly. "Why, write about your little Quaker girl, Cara, if she interests you so much."

"But I can't, Charles! That would be stealing from Mary Starbuck."

The Reverend Charles Snedeker shook his head, but he did not argue. "Does she have to live in Nantucket?" he asked instead.

Mrs. Snedeker thought about the suggestion contained in the question. Why, that was the solution, of course. Lay the scene of her story somewhere else. Here on Long Island, for instance, there was a whaling port where the little Quaker girl, member of a seafaring family, could easily live. She would go to that old whaling port at once and get material for her story.

But it was no use. The Quaker girl who had taken possession of her mind would not be transplanted. She belonged in Nantucket and she would live nowhere else. Mrs. Snedeker determined to forget the strong-willed child. She would write something different.

Early the next summer the Snedekers returned to Nantucket. And then Charles Snedeker had his say.

"I'm tired of all this fuss about a Nantucket story. You haven't forgotten that character who attracted you so, Cara, and you know you haven't."

"No," Mrs. Snedeker admitted. "I tried to forget her, but I couldn't. She isn't a child you can forget, Charles."

"Well, you just come with me," said her husband, taking her by the arm.

"Where are we going?"

"To Miss Starbuck's."

Mrs. Snedeker protested. She did not want to go. She did not want to tell her friend that she had been thinking of a story that belonged in the Nantucket woman's province. But she went with her husband, just the same.

Mr. Snedeker explained. Mrs. Snedeker blushed. But Miss Starbuck smiled.

"Why, of course you can write about Nantucket if you want to. Why not? Everybody does."

Mrs. Snedeker sighed with relief. At last she was

free to write about the child who had captured her imagination that day on Fair Street.

But the writer had no more than planned her story before her dear husband became ill. All of her time and thought and energy were for him, and writing was forgotten.

Mr. Snedeker died the following spring, and the world was empty. Even writing, which Mrs. Snedeker had always loved, seemed no longer possible, since she was accustomed to looking to her husband for encouragement and criticism. Time after time she tried to begin her story of Dencey, the little Quaker girl, but she could not write alone. She began to believe she would never write again.

Finally she went once more to Nantucket, and there at last she began to write. At first the book went slowly, but soon it was going faster and faster, for Dencey herself was taking things into her own hands and steering the story the way it ought to go. Mary Starbuck, the Snedekers' Nantucket friend, was constantly helpful and encouraging.

Downright Dencey was published in 1927 by Doubleday. Its success was immediate and lasting. Thanks to the vision which came to her on Fair Street and stayed with her in spite of discouragement and sorrow, Caroline Dale Snedeker proved to the world that she could write books of enduring worth, and to herself she proved that life held something for her, even though her beloved husband was gone.

31. *Seven Instead of One*

Abe Lincoln Grows Up — Sandburg, 1928

EVERY YOUNG AMERICAN should read *Abe Lincoln Grows Up*, the story of the boyhood of a well-loved American. Written simply and vividly, this biography makes Abe Lincoln live again, a real boy growing up to take his place in the world.

It is not strange that the author of this book was able to picture Lincoln so sympathetically and realistically, for he was well equipped for his task. His own boyhood had been much like that of the man he was writing about. All his life he had heard Lincoln anecdotes from neighbors who had known the great man. And for nearly twenty years before he began to write about Lincoln he had been gathering material. In fact, he gathered so much material and learned so much about his subject as he worked that the *one* book he planned to write on Abraham Lincoln's life turned into *seven!*

One day in 1923 two men sat at lunch in the Chatham Hotel in New York. One was Alfred Harcourt of Harcourt, Brace and Company; the other was Carl

Sandburg, poet, author, newspaper man, collector of folk songs, and lecturer extraordinary. The two had much to talk about, for months had passed since their last meeting, and aside from their business relation of publisher and author, they were good friends.

Over the soup Harcourt remarked, "Well, your two Rootabaga books are going well, Carl. I hope you have another juvenile up your sleeve."

Sandburg shook his head and, as usual, his hair fell into his eyes. "Nope. I'm full of Lincoln these days, Alf," he said, pushing his hair back. "Can't think of anything else."

Harcourt knew that his friend had been planning for years to write something about the great president and that he had been collecting books and pamphlets on Lincoln's times for almost as long.

"Have you decided yet," he asked now, "what you're going to do with your Lincoln stuff?"

"No, I haven't really decided, but I think maybe I'll do a short piece of about ten thousand words, putting the emphasis on his prairie background. You know, Alf, Lincoln was a great fellow, but he wasn't the plaster saint some of these politicians like to make us think. I want to break down all this sentimentalizing about him and show him as the genuine, down-to-earth sort of man he really was."

The soup plates were removed. The lunch proceeded, and the talk kept pace with it.

Over the entree one of the friends suddenly said, "Say! Why not a book for young people about Lincoln? There's never been a really good biography of him for boys and girls."

"That's an idea," agreed the other. "In fact, it's a splendid idea. How long a book. . . ."

By the time they had finished dessert, the friends had reached an agreement. Sandburg would submit an outline for a juvenile life of Lincoln which would run about four hundred book pages. Harcourt would go over the company's publishing program with the proposed biography in mind and would be ready with plans for publication.

When Carl Sandburg reached his home in a suburb of Chicago, he set to work in earnest on his life of Lincoln for boys and girls. With a young audience in mind, he wrote simply, directly, but with the beauty of style which he brought to any writing. When he had finished a few chapters, however, he began to doubt that he could write this book for children. There were heights and depths in the life of Lincoln which were beyond the comprehension of children. What, then, should he do? If he left out all that was too adult, too mature, he might make the book so simple it would have little meaning. On the other hand, if he wrote the biography in full, as he saw it, it would never appeal to boys and girls. At last he decided to drop the idea of writing for children and aim his book at adults instead.

The more he worked on the biography, the bigger Sandburg saw his task. In place of a short piece of about ten thousand words as he had first envisioned it, or a single book for young people, he soon realized that to do justice to a life of Lincoln he must write perhaps two big volumes.

Years of incredible labor followed. Sandburg worked night and day, sometimes straight around the clock. He spent hour after hour digging for facts in already published biographies, old newspapers, old letters and pamphlets; and then more hours writing down the facts and checking them against everything else he could find on the subject. He worked out a filing system of his own, in orange crates and boxes, with a big envelope for each item of Lincoln's life: one for "looks"; one for "speech"; one for "religion"; "Gettysburg Address"; "laughter"; "the White House when Lincoln lived there"; and so on.

His biography of Lincoln was not the only thing Sandburg had to do during those years, however. He was still working as a newspaper man on the *Chicago Daily News* and had to keep up with his assignments. He continued to write poetry. He added to his collection of folk songs which he had begun long before. And he still took time out occasionally to recite his poetry and sing folk songs before audiences in different parts of the country.

But Sandburg learned to make these time-consuming public appearances help in his work on Lincoln. When his wife showed him an invitation to speak and sing at a certain college, he would look up the school's location on the map and check that place with the data in his files before answering the letter. If he could find no indication that his trip would yield anything further about the life of Lincoln, he would reject the invitation, but if there was some old person in the vicinity who had known Lincoln, or if the town had a museum or a library which might be helpful, he would accept.

After filling his lecture engagement, he would remain in town a while, searching for Lincoln material. Everything he found he brought home and filed in his envelopes that filled an increasing number of boxes.

So the work went on. At last, in 1925, Sandburg finished two big volumes which he called *Abraham Lincoln: The Prairie Years*. They were published serially in the *Pictorial Review* and then as books, early in 1926. Immediately adults of America recognized in Sandburg's work a genuine, sympathetic but unsentimentalized biography of a great American.

Then Alfred Harcourt, who had published *The Prairie Years*, went back to his original idea of a life of Lincoln for children. Publisher and author soon saw that, with little change, the first twenty-seven chapters of *Abraham Lincoln: The Prairie Years* could stand alone as a book for young people. James Daugherty, whose vigorous style was especially appropriate for a book of frontier life, was asked to illustrate it.

So *Abe Lincoln Grows Up* was published, to become one of the favorite biographies of young America.

Sandburg was not yet through, however. By the time he finished *The Prairie Years* he knew that he must write more about Abraham Lincoln—but he had no idea how much more or how long it would take him. He continued to write for sixteen years before he completed his life of Lincoln! The finishing took four more huge volumes, which were published at last in 1939 under the title *Abraham Lincoln: The War Years.*

Thus the book which he had first thought to write as a single book for young people turned into seven volumes instead and established the name of Carl Sandburg as a great biographer as well as poet.

32. Extravagance that Paid

Hitty: Her First Hundred Years — Field, 1929

HITTY IS A real person in the world of books. As you read about her adventures, her misfortunes and her triumphs, you are as interested and anxious as if she were a real flesh-and-blood person, instead of a tiny doll made of a piece of ashwood. The story of Hitty's first hundred years is fascinating, from the day the peddler carved her and fastened her together with wooden pegs to the day she began to write her memoirs, sitting there in the antique shop. As one young reader put it, "I wish there was a book about Hitty's second hundred years."

It is no wonder that the little doll becomes a real character in her story, because the original Hitty made such an impression on the people who made the book that they bought her, though the price was far beyond their means.

It was a winter evening in 1928. Rachel Field, a writer of children's books, and her good friend, Dorothy Lathrop, an illustrator of children's books, had just dined together in a small shop on West Eighth

Street in New York City. Arm in arm, they strolled down the street, chatting happily. This was an evening to be enjoyed to the utmost, for the two friends did not see each other as often as they would have liked, since one lived in Albany and the other here in New York City.

"What shall we do now, Dorothy?" asked Miss Field. "Where would you like to go?"

"Let's stop and say good evening to Hitty," suggested Miss Lathrop.

"Hitty?" repeated Rachel Field, puzzled. "Who is she? I don't remember meeting anyone named Hitty. A new friend of yours, Dorothy?"

Dorothy Lathrop smiled. "Well, not exactly. In fact, she is a very old friend, though we have never spoken to each other."

The writer looked her bewilderment. The artist smiled again, and then hastened to enlighten her friend.

"Hitty is a doll, Rachel, a tiny, old-fashioned, wooden doll in an antique shop down the street a few doors. Her name is sewed inside her dress. For months I've— Why, Rachel, what's the matter?"

Rachel Field had stopped short, her mouth open in astonishment, her expressive eyes shining with excitement. "Dorothy! Do you mean to tell me that you, too, have been admiring my doll?"

"*Your* doll?"

"Well, not mine really. How I wish she were!" Rachel sighed longingly. "Oh, Dorothy, I've wanted so to buy that doll! I go past the shop and look and look at her. But I know she must be frightfully expensive—she's obviously a genuine antique. I've even been afraid to go inside the shop, for I know that if I did, I'd want her more than ever. And I just can't afford her."

"Then I'm braver than you," answered her friend. "This morning I went into the shop and asked what they wanted for the little doll. And Rachel! The price is staggering!" The artist named a figure which took her friend's breath away.

"O-oh!" Rachel sighed. "It's a good thing I didn't go in to look at her. I could never afford that."

"Nor I," agreed Miss Lathrop. "But it doesn't cost anything to *look* at her. Let's go and look through the window."

And the friends went on down the street to stand before the window of the antique shop and gaze at the little doll. What a fascinating little thing Hitty was! No more than six and a half inches high, dressed in an old-fashioned brown-sprigged calico dress, she looked much more like a person than a doll. Her little brown face, with its turned-up nose and its wide-apart eyes and unfathomable smile, had too much character for a mere doll. Hitty was a real personality.

The two friends stood for a long time outside the shop window, staring covetously at the doll. If only she were not so expensive! But, of course, she was a regular museum piece and genuine early American; she must be well over a hundred years old. The writer and the artist, both lovers of antiques, knew that one could not

expect to buy really old things without paying dearly
for them.

At last the friends turned regretfully away from the
window. What was the use of looking at something
they could not afford? Antiques are for the rich, and
young authors and illustrators should not waste their
time longing for them.

So Dorothy Lathrop returned to Albany and Rachel
Field went back to her New York home to settle down
to her writing.

In the following weeks, Rachel Field found many
excuses to go past that little shop on Eighth Street.
Each time she passed she stopped to look at the diminutive doll, and with each look the doll became more
desirable. Her enthusiasm mounted steadily. Frequently she wrote to her friend in Albany and in each
letter she told about Hitty: Hitty still sat in the window; Hitty continued to smile as New Yorkers hur-
ried past the shop; Hitty had not yet found anyone
she cared to live with.

But one day when Rachel Field paused in front of
the antique shop, she caught her breath and stared.
Hitty was not there! The little doll had been sold!
Now they would never see her again.

As Rachel went toward home with lagging steps, she
felt overwhelmingly sad. Perhaps it was ridiculous to
care so much about a little wooden doll, but the fact
remained that she did care tremendously. Somehow
she had never really believed that the doll would be
sold. Maybe she had thought no one would ever have

that much money to spend for six and a half inches of ashwood. But there it was: Hitty was gone. She might as well write the sad news to Dorothy.

By return mail she received an even more depressing answer.

"Oh, why didn't we buy Hitty when we had the chance!" wrote Dorothy Lathrop. "It just occurred to me the other day, Rachel, that while neither of us could afford—alone—to buy her, we might put our money together and buy her in partnership. Then she could never be taken away where we would never see her.

"If we had bought her, Rachel, we might have made a book about her. You could have done the story and I the pictures. But now it's too late. We'll never see Hitty again."

The letter ended with the suggestion that Rachel go into the antique shop and find out if the doll had really been sold.

Acting on her friend's advice, but feeling that it was useless, Rachel Field went into the antique shop. A dignified lady came forward to meet her.

"The doll," began Rachel timidly. "The doll you had in the window—"

The lady's face brightened. "Oh, you mean Hitty. Would you like to see her?"

"Would I like to see—" Rachel repeated, unbelieving. Then her expressive face glowed. "You mean—you still have her? She isn't sold?"

"Not yet." The lady turned to a desk and opened

a drawer. "Here she is. We took her out of the window the other day to show to a customer and forgot to put her back."

Rachel Field took the little doll carefully between her thumb and forefinger. This was destiny, she thought solemnly. It would seem that she and Dorothy were intended to do Hitty's story. It had taken their fear that the doll was sold to bring them to the point of making this seemingly extravagant purchase.

"I'll take her," she told the woman. "And I want her sent to Albany, to Dorothy P. Lathrop. . . ."

All the time she was purchasing the doll and watching the lady pack the little figure carefully in a box for shipment, Rachel Field's mind was busy with Hitty's story. She began to know, as if Hitty herself had told her, some things which had happened to the doll in her hundred years of existence. That brown complexion was undoubtedly once much fairer; it had been darkened on a whaling voyage Hitty had taken in her youth with a family from—why, from Maine, of course, named . . . Preble was the name without a doubt. Since Hitty had lived over a hundred years, she had seen trains take the place of stagecoaches and she had watched steamboats supplant sailing vessels. She had seen . . .

"And what is the address, please?"

Rachel Field woke out of her trance. The antique shop owner was speaking to her. The doll was packed, ready to go.

Miss Field gave the woman Dorothy Lathrop's address and went home to dream some more about Hitty's adventures.

That was the beginning of Hitty's book. For weeks the two friends wrote each other all the things they felt sure must have happened to their little doll. They consulted Louise Seaman, their editor at The Macmillan Company, who added her enthusiasm and imagination to theirs.

That summer, they went—taking Hitty, of course—to the little island off the coast of Maine which was Rachel Field's favorite summer residence. There the story of Hitty's first hundred years became plainer and fuller. For a week the writer and illustrator talked of nothing but Hitty, until finally they felt they knew her story as well as if they had actually been with her all through those hundred years.

After the artist returned to her home, Rachel began to write. As she finished a chapter or two, she sent the manuscript to Dorothy to make the pictures. So through the following months, the history of Hitty was written and illustrated.

In 1929 The Macmillan Company published *Hitty: Her First Hundred Years*. It was immediately popular. The following year the book earned for Rachel Field the Newbery Medal—she was the first woman to receive this award.

So it was that the extravagance of Rachel Field and Dorothy Lathrop in buying an antique doll they could not afford paid them richly in pleasure, in honor, and in money.

33. *Never Too Late*

Little House In the Big Woods — Wilder, 1932

ARE LAURA AND Mary and Almanzo dear friends of yours? If not, then you are to be both pitied and envied. You are to be pitied because you have missed all this time the pleasure which thousands of American children have found in reading about the way boys and girls lived two generations ago, and envied because you have before you the thrill that comes when first you read about Laura and her family and friends. No matter what your age, you are neither too young nor too old to enjoy Laura Ingalls Wilder's series of stories. A word of warning, however: if you are going to read them, you might as well begin with the first one, *The Little House in the Big Woods*, for if you start with one of the later ones, you will undoubtedly want to know what went before. Eventually you will read them all, so you had better begin with the first one and go right on through to the last, *These Happy Golden Years*.

This series of true stories about real people is one of the most popular with boys and girls ever written, because each book is a good story, absorbing from the first page to the last, with characters who become well-loved friends. And the books are equally popular with the adults who choose books for children, because they are more than good entertainment: they are an education in American ideals. Yet these excellent books would never have been written if their author had been willing to accept the convention which decrees that a person's creative life is over when middle age is passed.

In 1932 Laura Ingalls Wilder was sixty-five years old. She had had a busy and active life. Before she was sixteen she had begun teaching school. At eighteen she had married a farmer, and the years which followed were full ones indeed, with the manifold duties of farmer's wife and devoted mother to crowd each day to the brim, plus the worries and suffering brought by seven years of drought, serious illness, the loss of their son, and the burning of their house.

The last few years, however, on their two-hundred-acre farm near Mansfield, Missouri, had been relatively peaceful and free from want, with the farm prospering and her husband Almanzo well and happy. But there was always plenty to keep Mrs. Wilder busy, with a ten-room farmhouse to look after, chickens to care for, churning and cooking and cleaning to do, besides the many farm women's clubs she had organized and the Mansfield Farm Loan Association she had managed for years.

Yes, at sixty-five, Laura Ingalls Wilder could truthfully say, if she cared to, that she had lived a full and active and useful life. Her daughter was grown, her work ended—so most people felt. Now she was surely entitled to a few years of rest and ease.

But nothing was farther from her thoughts. Instead of cutting down on her work, now that she was past middle-age, Mrs. Wilder took on more work. She began to write.

At first she wrote short articles for farm magazines, then special articles for national magazines. Everything she wrote was accepted for publication, and she began to be recognized as an expert on farm topics.

But another sort of writing had been beckoning to this white-haired beginner. For years Mrs. Wilder had wanted to write down the stories her father had told his daughters about his childhood.

What a wonderful storyteller Pa had been! Mrs. Wilder remembered his stories vividly. She could hear him now, his rich, gay voice; she could see his vital, expressive face. And then his fiddle—his precious Amati —would she ever forget the music of that fiddle? Through the years the golden notes came echoing down to her, telling her, as they had when she used to listen to them as a child, that life was good, no matter what danger threatened or trouble brewed.

More and more, as she went about her work straining milk, feeding chickens, going for the mail, writing farm articles, playing cribbage in the evenings with Almanzo, Laura Wilder wished that she could preserve for future generations Pa's stories. It would be a shame to let them be forgotten. Perhaps she should write her autobiography. She decided to try.

However, she soon abandoned the autobiography. It did not satisfy her. Such a book would be read by adults, and it was children she wanted to reach. Pa's stories belonged to the boys and girls of America, because they were about the life of children in an earlier America, when boys and girls had less of material riches than the average child of today, but more of security and genuine happiness than many young people know in this busy, hurrying twentieth century. Yes, she would write for children.

So, when she had a free moment between farm chores, Mrs. Wilder began her story. In a big, rough school tablet she wrote with a pencil, "Once upon a time, sixty years ago, a little girl lived in the Big Woods—" Memories, living memories, crowded in upon her, memories of her own childhood and of Pa's stories about his.

Day after day, when time permitted, she kept on writing in the big tablet. When it was filled, she began another. And then another. Soon she had enough for a book.

After working over her material painstakingly, revising and polishing it and verifying dates, she copied it and sent it to a publisher.

Mrs. Wilder was not particularly surprised when her manuscript was accepted the first time out. (She had never had anything refused and did not realize that many writers try over and over again before they succeed in getting their work accepted.) But she was

NEVER TOO LATE   181

deeply pleased. Now Pa's stories would not be forgotten. Now other children would enjoy them as she, too, had loved them as a child. Now she could stop writing. Her self-appointed task was finished.

But Mrs. Wilder soon found that she could not stop. When *The Little House in the Big Woods* was published, children all over the country loved it immediately. They took Laura and Mary and Carrie to their hearts. And they wanted to know more about them. Letters began to come to Mrs. Wilder asking, "What happened next? Please tell us."

Then other memories crowded upon her—memories of pioneer days in new country, in the prairies of western Kansas and South Dakota, and in Minnesota. She remembered hardships that were somehow not hardships because of the spirit in which they were faced. She remembered the work and struggle that went into making a new country safe and civilized.

So Mrs. Wilder wrote another book to tell what happened next. . . . And then another. . . . And another. . . . And so on until she had finished the story of Laura's childhood.

Laura Ingalls Wilder made her own wish come true. Her Pa's stories will never be forgotten so long as there are children to read her books. But more than that, Pa himself will never be forgotten, nor will Ma or Laura or Mary or Almanzo or any of the other people who live in Mrs. Wilder's books as they lived in her own early life. Furthermore, Laura Ingalls Wilder proved that it is never too late to do something that is worth doing.

34. *The Introduction That Became a Book*

Invincible Louisa—Meigs, 1933

LOUISA MAY ALCOTT was not only a writer of some of the world's best-loved books for boys and girls; she was a woman of fine character and indomitable will, whose life has been an inspiration to many who have followed her.

Invincible Louisa is a living picture of this splendid writer of an earlier day. It was written by a woman who herself knew what a source of inspiration and courage Louisa Alcott's life could be. Without doubt, the book owes much of its excellence to the fact that the author wanted to pass on this knowledge to the young people of today. And it was written because she was asked to write an introduction.

By 1930 Cornelia Meigs was an established writer for young people; her stories of early days in America were read and loved all over the country.

One day she received a request from Little, Brown &

Company, who had published some of her books. Since the centenary of Louisa May Alcott was approaching, Little, Brown (who had bought out Miss Alcott's publishers) were planning to issue a bibliography of that famous writer's works. Would Miss Meigs write an introduction for the bibliography?

Miss Meigs would be glad, indeed, to write the introduction. All her life she had loved Louisa Alcott's books for boys and girls. Moreover, Ednah D. Cheney's book, *Louisa May Alcott: Her Life, Letters, and Journals*, had been her favorite book as far back as she could remember, as it had been her mother's favorite before her. How much help and inspiration they had found in that book, both the mother and the daughter. When problems seemed too difficult to solve, when troubles seemed too much to bear, they would often turn the pages of Louisa Alcott's *Life and Letters* and draw strength and hope from the unswerving faith and unfailing courage of that brave soul. Yes, it would be a labor of love to write an introduction for the bibliography of Miss Alcott's works, a hundred years after her birth.

But when Cornelia Meigs took down her well-worn copy of *Louisa May Alcott: Her Life, Letters, and Journals* and went over it again, she was struck by the biography's incompleteness, its inadequacy. Published in 1889, just a year after Miss Alcott's death, the book was an excellent biography for its time. But readers of this day and age want to know a great deal more about a person than biographers of the 1880's thought it necessary to tell.

As the days passed, Miss Meigs found herself postponing the writing of the requested introduction. Instead, she was thinking about writing an entire book —a new life of Louisa May Alcott, one which would present her to modern readers as a living person, whom they could understand and sympathize with, from whom they could draw inspiration. Would Little, Brown & Company be interested, she wondered, in letting her undertake the writing of such a book?

She had her answer soon. One of the Little, Brown editors came to see her. At the first break in the conversation, Miss Meigs started to suggest that she would like to write a biography of Louisa May Alcott for young people, but before she could get the words out, the editor said,

"I wonder, Miss Meigs, if you would undertake a life of Miss Alcott? For young people, of course."

Cornelia Meigs stared incredulously at the editor a moment, and then she smiled. "Why, I was just going to suggest the very same thing!"

The editor smiled back. "You'll do it, then?"

"I will try," agreed the author. "I can't think of any book I'd rather write."

So Cornelia Meigs began work on the book which was to be both the pleasantest to write and the most rewarding of any she had ever done. She read everything she could find about Louisa May Alcott. With the help of her publishers, she visited and talked with many old people who remembered Miss Alcott and her father, and Emerson and Thoreau and Hawthorne. And then she met Mrs. Pratt, the daughter-in-law of Anna Alcott, who was "Meg" in *Little Women*. Mrs. Pratt gave her much information which had never been published. In addition, Cornelia Meigs' own lifelong love and admiration for Louisa Alcott helped her to make this biography the best of her many good books.

When *Invincible Louisa* was published in 1933, it was immediately recognized as a splendid biography for young people. The following year it was awarded the Newbery Medal. With the income she received from royalties, Miss Meigs bought a farm in Vermont, with a big house she had long wanted to have so that her beloved nieces and nephews could stay with her as often and as long as they liked.

Thus Cornelia Meigs received both recognition and profit from the book which grew out of a proposed introduction. But she always said the honor should go to Louisa, for the book was really a collaboration with her.

35. Remembered Yesterdays

Caddie Woodlawn — Brink, 1935

CADDIE WOODLAWN, MADCAP tomboy, fearless, wilful, honest. Caddie riding to warn the Indians. Caddie playing practical jokes on their guest from the East. Caddie growing at last to a knowledge of the beauty and worth of womanhood.

If you have read *Caddie Woodlawn*, you will never forget her. You will remember, too, whether you realize it or not, a great deal about pioneer days in Wisconsin, and that was what the author wanted you to do. She wrote the book because she felt that boys and girls of today should know something about the pioneer age that has passed. She wanted the children of today to remember the yesterdays of their grandparents.

Carol Ryrie Brink, with her family, was spending the winter of 1933 in France. While her husband, a mathematics professor on leave from the University of Minnesota, was studying and her children were in school, she was accustomed to amuse herself in her spare time by writing. Many of her stories and poems had been

published in the last few years and she had just finished
a book, *Anything Can Happen on the River.* Now she
was trying to decide what to work on next. Should it
be a short story, a poem, or a book?

While she was wondering about this, Mrs. Brink
received a letter from her grandmother in Idaho. En-
closed with the letter was a newspaper clipping which
told of the death of a Wisconsin Indian, called "Indian
John," at the age of 110.

"I feel sure," the letter said, "that this was the Indian
John I knew as a child. You remember the stories I used
to tell you about him, don't you?"

Carol Brink looked up from the letter. Did she remember the stories Grandmother used to tell about her
childhood in Wisconsin! Would she ever forget them?
What a wonderful storyteller her grandmother was!
And what a lovable, hoydenish girl Caddie Woodhouse
must have been!

Through the days that followed, Carol Brink found
herself thinking of those tales of hardships and adventures the Woodhouse family had experienced out there
in Wisconsin when it was still wild backwoods. Though
she had never met them, Carol Brink felt she knew each
one of her grandmother's brothers and sisters very well
indeed through those stories. In families where there
is no one who can tell stories of pioneer days, the children certainly miss a lot, Mrs. Brink was sure.

And then came the thought: why not write a book
about her grandmother's childhood—a book for children? She could weave into a story all those anecdotes

she had heard as a little girl. Caddie Woodhouse, an old women now, was still living in Idaho and could supply any details she required. Yes, she would do it. And she would write to her grandmother right now—this very minute—and tell her what she meant to do.

That was the beginning of the series of letters and questionnaires which, during the following months, passed between Idaho, U.S.A., and Paris, France. As Mrs. Brink considered her book idea, she thought of more and more things she wanted to know: what kind of clothes had they worn when her grandmother was a child? What slang did they use? What were the furnishings like in the sitting room? What kind of vegetables did they raise? How did the Indians dress?

Each question she thought of was jotted down, and periodically a list of them was sent to Idaho. In due time the answers came back and Carol Brink was usually ready with more questions.

All during the winter this voluminous correspondence continued. By the time the Brinks returned to their home in Minnesota in the spring, the writer felt that she knew the people of her grandmother's family and their way of life well enough to begin her book.

But there was the matter of background. She knew northern Wisconsin well, because for years the Brinks had spent most of their summers in a cottage in the backwoods there, but she was not familiar with the particular section where the young Caddie had lived. She wanted to see for herself the old farm where the adventures of her grandmother's stories had taken place. But would she be able to find it after all these years? And if she did find it, would it not be so changed by the passing of nearly three-quarters of a century that seeing it would do her no good?

Well, she had to try. Accordingly, one week end in May, Carol Brink and her husband set out to find the old farm where Caddie and her family had lived.

It was a beautiful drive. The wild cherries were in blossom and hepaticas were opening in the woods. As the Brinks drove, they talked.

"It's probably a wild goose chase, Carol," remarked her husband cheerfully, "but at least it will set your mind at rest."

"Grandmother wrote me the directions," Carol answered, taking the letter out of her purse. "Let's see: she says, 'one-half mile from Dunnville school.' We'll have to locate the school first. And then she says, 'There's a turn in the road at the end of a long hill.'"

Raymond Brink laughed heartily. "And you expect to find the place with directions like those! Remember, dear, it has been over sixty years—"

"Almost seventy," Carol corrected him.

"Almost seventy, then, since your grandmother has seen this place. Everything is sure to be changed."

"I guess you're right," sighed Mrs. Brink. "We'll never find the old place by these directions. . . . But couldn't we look up old tax records and find the legal descriptions or something?"

Her husband nodded. "That's the sensible course, Carol. We'll go to the courthouse first thing."

So the Brinks drove to the county seat and looked up old tax records. In short order, they found the description of the old Woodhouse farm. Once they reached Dunnville, it would be a simple matter to locate the place.

But Dunnville itself was difficult to find. The town had almost disappeared. When the Brinks thought they must be near the town, they asked a rural mail carrier, "How far is it to Dunnville?"

"You're in the middle of it right now," he answered.

The Brinks looked around dumbfounded. No one would ever guess that this quiet country lane was the middle of a town!

The schoolhouse was still there, however, and just for fun, as they drove out to the farm, Carol checked the route with the directions her grandmother had given her. At the schoolhouse she noted the mileage on the speedometer. Soon she saw the turn in the road at the end of a long hill. Yes, and there was the farm! Part of the house had been torn down; the big barn had been replaced by a smaller one; the four pine trees which the children had planted so many years ago had been cut down; but still it was the Woodhouse farm.

As they drew up at the gate, the speedometer showed just half a mile from the Dunnville school.

"Look, Raymond," Carol Brink laughed, "we could have found it with grandmother's directions, after all!"

For hours they wandered around the farm and talked with the present owners. Everywhere she turned, Carol found herself remembering one of her grandmother's

stories. There was the river, the lake, the woods—
everything as her grandmother had described them.
Carol felt as if she, herself, had lived here and remembered those years, instead of knowing them only
through someone else.

At last the Brinks went back to the car, after getting
from the present residents the name of an aged settler
in a neighboring town who might remember the Wood-
houses.

As they drove off, Carol looked back at the old farm,
so little changed by the years.

"And we really found it!" she marveled.

Raymond shook his head. "I can't believe it, that a
place could stay the same for so many years, untouched
by civilization."

"Why do you suppose it is?"

"Probably a matter of transportation. When your
grandmother lived here, Carol, there was a lot of traffic
on the river. Naturally they supposed the country
around here would build up. Instead, river traffic
declined. And the railroads passed them by. So this
section was left, high and dry, just as it was years ago."

Later the Brinks talked to old settlers. They heard
many stories of bygone days when Caddie was a girl.
Caddie's childhood became clearer than ever in Carol
Brink's mind, and she knew it would make a good book.

Back home again, she began writing. The hardest
part was deciding how to start. She had a great deal
of material—far too much, she feared, for one book.
But her material had no plot; it did not hang together.

Yet she wanted her book about Caddie to be not only a true picture of the period, but a continuous, absorbing story as well. How should she begin?

Then she remembered how Caddie and her brothers used to cross the river. That would be a good starting place—a typical prank of the tomboy Caddie.

Once under way, the story fell into line. Many of her grandmother's tales she found she could weave in satisfactorily. Some she was forced to leave out. Occasionally she had to make up a few bits to round out the story. But in the main, her book was the real Caddie's book—a story of the young Caddie and her family in long-ago Wisconsin.

As she did with all her books, Carol Brink read the story to her own children, fifteen-year-old David and eight-year-old Nora. They were fascinated with it. They liked stories of the old days as much as she had, herself, when she was a child.

When *Caddie Woodlawn* was finished, after two years of work, it was accepted immediately by The Macmillan Company, and published in 1935. The following year it received the Newbery Award. Naturally, that honor pleased Carol Brink. But what pleased her most was her grandmother's delight in *Caddie Woodlawn* and the knowledge that the remembered yesterdays of the real Caddie would never be forgotten.

36. From Tiny Acorns

The Yearling — Rawlings, 1938

HAVE YOU EVER had a pet you loved? Then you can understand how Jody felt about Flag, his pet deer. You know how hard it was for him to have to . . . But if you have read *The Yearling*, you know all about it, and if you haven't read it, then you will want to find out for yourself what happened.

The Yearling is one of the outstanding books of our time for boys and girls. Yet it was not written for children. It grew, slowly and gradually, from a memory of a single day in the author's life, and that author thought so little of the book while she was writing it that frequently she was ready to throw the manuscript away.

When, in 1928, Marjorie Kinnan Rawlings, writer, bought a grove of 2500 orange trees at Cross Creek, in northern Florida, she knew she had found the spot which would mean home to her for the rest of her life. In a short time she had also found the people and the country she wanted to write about. Her succeeding books, *South Moon Under* and *Golden Apples*, established her name among adult readers as a writer of promise.

Those early years in Florida were busy ones. Mrs. Rawlings worked hard to build up a productive orange grove. Her task was complicated by poison ivy, roaming livestock, drunk or crazy farm hands, poisonous snakes, neighborhood feuds, freezes, termites—it seemed that no sooner had she overcome one difficulty than another obstacle reared its head. But each time she managed to win out sufficiently to make a modest profit from her grove.

Writing took time, too, and plenty of hard work. When she was writing a book, Mrs. Rawlings spent eight hours a day at her typewriter, whether she wrote two pages a day or six lines.

Being a friend and neighbor took time, too. There was always someone needing help, or there were social affairs she must attend if she did not wish to offend her neighbors, or there was good crabbing weather, or the fish were biting. All in all it was a busy life, but very rich and satisfying.

For a long time a story idea had been in Mrs. Rawlings' mind. She remembered vividly a certain April day in her own childhood when her world seemed breathtakingly lovely; yet at the height of her joy in her beautiful, carefree life she realized suddenly that she could not always be a child. Soon she would grow up; and with that growing up would come responsibilities; her happy, carefree childhood would be over.

For years Mrs. Rawlings had intended to write a

story, some day, about the joy of childhood and the realization of coming maturity. Now, as she came to know and love the wild scrub country of northern Florida near her home, she decided to use this country for the background of her story. As she became acquainted with her neighbors and went hunting and fishing and exploring with them, she made notes on the wild life of the country; she talked to the old hunters about their early days in the scrub; and she began to amass background material for her story.

But still she had no real story; she had no particular characters in mind; there was only that long-treasured memory of what a magic April day meant to a child, and a lot of information about what life in the scrub country was like.

Then Mrs. Rawlings lived for a while in the heart of the scrub with an old-timer in the district, Cal Long, and his wife. The writer and the old hunter worked side by side, hauling wood and sawing it, hunting bears that killed the stock, and chasing foxes out of the corn-field. Often, especially in the evenings, the old man talked about his childhood in this place. His family had been poor, as nearly everyone in the scrub was poor. Life was hard, and every member of the family had to work to grow food to live on. Yet Cal did not complain as he told of his difficult boyhood. To him such a life seemed natural and inevitable.

Only one thing about those long-ago years caused him grief. "I had me a pet deer," he said. "Sweetest little thing you ever see. Followed me like a dog, that deer did. I thought a heap of it."

The old man fell silent. Mrs. Rawlings waited a moment, and then she asked, "What happened? Did you keep it?"

Old Cal shook his head sadly. "Time it grew to yearling size, it could jump any fence a feller could build. One time it jumped the fence into the cornfield."

Again the old man was silent, remembering. Mrs. Rawlings knew what he was seeing. She knew what a yearling deer would do to a corn crop and she realized what the corn crop had meant to Cal's family—their livelihood.

At last the old man said, "My pa made me shoot it. He made me kill my pet deer that loved me." Although more than half a century had passed since that day, the memory still brought pain to the old man's eyes. "All my life," he said, "it's hurted me."

When Mrs. Rawlings went to bed that night, she knew she had her story at last. The child in her story would be such a boy as Old Cal and the other old-timers she had talked to had been; he would have just such a hard life in the wild scrub country. And a pet deer, which he loved with all his boy's heart, would be the means of precipitating him from childhood into maturity. She would tell the story of a year in that boy's life.

So, after years of thinking about it, and more years of gathering background material, Mrs. Rawlings began to write her story of *The Yearling*. It took another year in the writing, and all through that year the author wondered if what she was writing was worth the effort. Many times she was tempted to toss the manuscript into the canal in which the gardener dumped his prunings and dead flowers. But she stuck to her task and at last the book was finished.

Immediately on its publication by Charles Scribner's Sons, *The Yearling* was chosen by the Book-of-the-Month Club as one of its selections. It won the Pulitzer Prize in fiction. It topped the best-seller list for years. All over the country adults read *The Yearling* and loved it.

Then boys and girls began to read it. Soon they claimed it as their own. So the book which grew out of the memory of a single day—the book which the author had felt was worthless and hopeless—became one of those rare books which are loved and remembered by children and grown-ups alike.

37. *The Frame That Came to Life*

Adam Of the Road — Gray, 1942

SEVEN CENTURIES AGO the world was very different
from today in transportation and communication, education and enlightenment. But people were much the
same and had much the same problems. Read *Adam
Of the Road*. Though he traveled on foot (except when
he was lucky enough to have a horse), though letters
were sent by messenger, and there was no such thing
as a public school, Adam was the sort of boy you might
meet today—resourceful, brave, loyal, and ambitious—
the kind of boy you would like to have for a friend.

Adam Of the Road, which presents a vivid picture of
life in thirteenth-century England, was written in
twentieth-century America by a woman who later became the teacher of the son of Japan's emperor. The
book owes its genuineness to the fact that the author
obeyed a mysterious compulsion to visit places which
she had no conscious wish to see.

It was the year 1939, in Germantown, Pennsylvania.
Elizabeth Gray Vining, who for years had written

books for boys and girls under her maiden name of
Elizabeth Janet Gray, was in the hospital recovering
from a serious illness. Her new book, *Penn*, had
recently been published. When she recovered her
strength, she meant to start another book . . . although
what the next one would be she had no idea.

One afternoon a friend—a schoolteacher—came to
see her. During the brief visit, the teacher spoke of
some trouble she was having with her work.

"We're studying the Middle Ages at school," she
said. "And it is so hard to find good material! About
medieval England, especially, there is just nothing."

After her visitor left, Mrs. Vining lay there, thinking. Her caller's words had reminded her of some work
she had done years before on the metrical romances of
the Middle Ages. How vividly she remembered that
work! Memories flooded the quiet hospital room.

It was during the glowing years of her brief, happy
marriage, before the accident which had taken her husband's life. The Vinings were in New York that year
while her husband worked for his degree at Columbia
University. He was studying metrical romances for his
middle English credit, and Mrs. Vining studied them
also, to keep him company. It was a lot of fun, working together. They had been unbelievably happy.

Mrs. Vining had found the poems so fascinating that
she planned to translate them for a book. She would
have a couple of wandering minstrels (perhaps a minstrel and his son) as a frame for the romances. Minstrels could find their way into all levels of society of

the period; they would suit their tales to their audiences. In that way, many different stories could be used.

Accordingly, Elizabeth Gray Vining began to translate the metrical romances of the Middle Ages. But soon she ran into trouble; the minstrels who told the tales began to occupy more of her attention than their stories. If that kept on, it would destroy her entire plan. She decided to drop the work and she put the whole thing away. It had been on the shelf, forgotten, all these years until her visitor's remark today about medieval England had reminded her of it.

All afternoon and evening, in the quiet intervals of hospital routine, Mrs. Vining's mind went back to that long-abandoned project of the minstrels and their tales.

That night, as had been usual lately, she could not get to sleep. About one o'clock, a boy she had never seen walked into her mind: a boy dressed in the doublet and hose of thirteenth-century England, a tousle-headed, snub-nosed, wide-mouthed, freckle-faced boy, with his harp over his shoulders and his dog at his heels. Throughout the remainder of the sleepless night, Mrs. Vining saw that boy walking the roads of medieval England, having adventures and making friends. He was a minstrel's son—no doubt about it; and he was as clear in her mind as if she had seen him day after day on the streets of Germantown.

Suddenly Mrs. Vining knew that she was going to write that book about thirteenth-century minstrels, after all; but it would be about Adam, the minstrel's son, and not about the romances of the Middle Ages. Instead of being part of the frame, Adam would be the story.

And now Mrs. Vining understood the explanation of a queer thing which had happened to her nearly three years before. She had been in England at the time, gathering material for her biography of William Penn. She wanted to visit the places Penn knew. She wanted to feel herself back in the England of his day, so that she could write about his life with confidence and authority.

But she found it impossible to keep to the program she had outlined for herself. Now and then she felt absolutely impelled to see places which had nothing whatever to do with Penn; and these were always places which had been centers of interest in the Middle Ages, centuries before Penn had lived. Some curious inner compulsion kept making her stop to see ancient inns, medieval churches, very old houses. Once she had even walked five miles to visit a sleepy little village which dated from the thirteenth-century; it had no place whatever on her schedule, but somehow she had felt satisfied after seeing it.

So it had gone all through Mrs. Vining's months in England. While her conscious mind was thinking about William Penn and gathering material about him, all the time a part of her mind, buried too deep for recognition, kept calling her attention to relics of the Middle Ages. She was intensely aware of three periods of time in England: the twentieth century of the present time with the coronation of the new king, Edward VIII; the eighteenth century of Penn's time, with its religious persecution and political turmoil; and the thirteenth century, the age of minstrelsy, the time of the beginning of freedom of learning and thought and speech. It was a strange feeling.

Almost three years had passed since then. Now, lying in her narrow hospital bed, Elizabeth Gray Vining understood why she had been so impelled to see everything she could which concerned thirteenth-century England. She saw why she had been driven, while in England, to see places and things which had no connection with the book she was writing at the time: she had had to find out what thirteenth-century life was like so that she could write the story of this minstrel's son who wandered over England during the Middle Ages.

Thus *Adam Of the Road* was written and became one of the most popular books of Elizabeth Janet Gray. Adam, who had been intended merely as a frame for old romances, came to life in the author's mind to make his long-ago world live for modern boys and girls.

38. *Triple Reward*

Johnny Tremain — Forbes, 1943

You HAVE READ about George Washington, Thomas
Jefferson, Paul Revere, Samuel Adams, and the other
men who were active during the American Revolution
which marked the beginning of our country. Have you
ever wondered what boys and girls were like during
those difficult years, what they did and thought, and
how they felt about the events of that critical period?
Johnny Tremain gives an excellent picture of one
boy's life and thoughts and feelings in that exciting
time, and it is an absorbing story as well. It was written by a woman who had never before written anything for boys and girls, and it was done as a reward
to herself for a well-kept promise.

Esther Forbes had been writing ever since she could
remember. Even as a child she had helped her older
brothers and sisters publish a neighboorhood magazine.
She had begun her first novel at the age of thirteen. In
fact, by the time she was grown she had written and
stored away—never to be published—more unfinished

novels, stories and plays than many authors write during an entire lifetime.

In 1940, she was an established writer, with several excellent historical novels published and selling well. And now she was trying something different—a straight biography which would have absolutely no fiction in it. She was writing the life of Paul Revere and she had vowed she would use nothing which was not a matter of record. She would not make up a single detail or imagine a single scene or a scrap of conversation. This book was going to be completely authentic, entirely objective—fact, not fiction. That was her resolution, and she was determined to stick to it.

But, oh, how hard it was sometimes! When she was gathering material about Paul Revere's father, for instance. The known facts about him were so sparse, so bare. He came to this country as a refugee; he became an apprentice to a certain man; when his son Paul was old enough, he took him into his shop as an apprentice in turn; he died— It was all completely bare and bleak. None of it gave any indication of what kind of man Appollos Revere was. Esther Forbes, biographer, would have loved to imagine a character for him, so that she could picture him as a living, breathing person. But she could not; she had resolved not to make up anything in writing this book. However, she promised herself that sometime she would write a book about that period and make up anything she liked, so long as it was typical of the time.

One day, Esther Forbes sat in her big, comfortable

home in Worcester, Massachusetts (the house where she was born), working on her biography of Paul Revere. She had come to the point where, at nineteen, Paul had suddenly enlisted to fight the French, although since his father's recent death he was in charge of the shop and responsible for the livelihood of his widowed mother and six younger children. As usual, Miss Forbes' mother, Harriette Merrifield Forbes (herself an authority on early New England history), had gathered together for her daughter all the source material she could find on that particular period of Paul Revere's life. Carefully, thoughtfully, Esther Forbes went through every record, every letter, trying to find the answer to the question in her mind: why did young Paul Revere leave home at that particular time, instead of staying at home and minding his trade? Nothing in all of the records gave a clue to the answer.

Finally, in exasperation, Esther Forbes said to her mother, "Why do you suppose Paul Revere left his silversmith trade to fight the French? Didn't he know it was a risk to leave his shop without adequate supervision?"

"Maybe his mother was bossing him too much," Mrs. Forbes answered with a smile.

"But didn't he care what happened to his mother and his brothers and sisters? What if things went badly while he was gone and they had no money to live on?"

Her mother nodded thoughtfully. "But perhaps he was so patriotic that he believed the good of the country came before the welfare of his family."

"Or maybe he was just tired of a humdrum, work-aday life," countered Esther Forbes.

"Or he might have been disappointed in love," put in her mother, "and wanted to show the girl she had refused a hero."

Miss Forbes sighed. "I wish I knew. I'd like to tell *why* he enlisted. But there's no indication in any of the material we've found as to the reason, so I suppose I shall just have to say he did it, and that's all." She picked up her pen, ready to write again, but stopped and looked at her mother. "Some day I'm going to write a story about boys of Paul Revere's time and tell not merely *what* was done but *why*. Sometime . . ."

The more she worked on the biography, the stronger became her desire to write a story about boys of the Revolution. The apprentices of the period particularly interested her. It was the custom for a boy to be apprenticed at an early age to a master craftsman; that was the only way trades were taught, for there were no technical schools then. And apprenticeship was closely akin to slavery, though it was only for a few years. A boy was completely at the mercy of his master. Some masters were kind, some were cruel; but apprentices took the kind they got and made the best of it. How interesting it would be to know how boys felt about their masters, and what effect the master-apprentice relationship had on their lives! Well, some-time. . . .

And so it went, on through her work on the monumental biography of Paul Revere. Time and again she came across an incident or a situation which challenged her imagination, but imagination was the one thing she was not using in this book. She filed such things away in her mind with the renewed promise that "sometime she would write a book in which she could imagine anything she liked, so long as it was true to the times."

At last her book was finished. *Paul Revere and the World He Lived In* was published. Now she was free to keep her promise to herself. Now she could write a book and give her imagination free rein.

Then came December 7, 1941. Pearl Harbor. America was at war. The youth of our country would be called on to fight. Boys who had been considered children in peace time would now be men, with a man's work and a man's responsibility. And suddenly Esther Forbes saw exactly what she wanted to do in this new book about Revolutionary times: she wanted to show boys in their teens what boys of the same age were up against at the time of the American Revolution, for the success of wars rests heavily on the sense of responsibility and manliness of young men.

The day after Pearl Harbor, Esther Forbes began her story about Johnny Tremain, the silversmith apprentice of Revolutionary times. She had little additional research to do. Not only had she become well acquainted with the times she was writing about through her work on *Paul Revere*, but from early childhood she had been thoroughly steeped in the history of New England, since she came of a long line of pre-Revolutionary ancestors, and both her parents were enthusiastic historians. All that remained was to interpret the facts she knew so well. So Johnny Tremain began to live and breathe and grow in the pages of his book.

Johnny Tremain was finished, and published in 1943 by Houghton Mifflin Company. The following year it was awarded the Newbery Medal for the year's most outstanding book for boys and girls, as *Paul Revere and the World He Lived In* had received, after its publication, the Pulitzer Prize as the best work of history for adults. Thus the spartan self-control which Esther Forbes exercised in keeping *Paul Revere* a straight, factual biography, with no imaginative touches, earned a triple reward for the author: the Pulitzer Prize for adults, the Newbery Award for children (she was the only person so far who had received both honors), and the joy of reaching an audience of young people. Truly a rich reward.